PRAISE FOR
THE COLOR OF COURAGE

"I love this book's balance of vulnerability, honesty, and readability. Anyone, at any level in Corporate America, will relate to the characters described in this book. You will be crushed and inspired by each chapter, and you'll also receive practical advice and tools about how to show up to the work of racial justice. Cindi is a gifted storyteller, as well as a practiced strategist. As an educator, I recommend purchasing a copy for each member of your work team and then forming a reading group, so you can unpack and debrief each chapter together."

–Erin Jones, Independent Education and Systems Consultant, Public Speaker

"Cindi Bright lays out her unfiltered story of oppressive Corporate norms and how they play out in everyday working life. As if talking to a friend over a glass of wine, *Color of Courage* leaves the reader no option but to self reflect on the role each of us plays in perpetuating racism in America."

–Frances Dewing, Cybersecurity & Tech industry leader

"You can't dismantle what you cannot see. This eye-opener book unveils the mechanics of racism and toxicity in Corporate America. A must-read for any leader serious about creating inclusive cultures."

–Venus Rekow, CEO, Neural Shifts

"This book is a must-read, not only for those enduring inequity, but for those unaware of the deep-seated, systemic, structural forces that drive these inequities. Through candid and engaging examples, and sometimes brutally honest dialogue, Cindi takes us to a place of practicality and comfort in calling out racist and bullying tactics, along with enforcing both institutional and individual accountability and change. If you have had enough waiting for reform and are interested in seeing results, this is the book for you."

–Asha Pillai, MD, Associate Professor of Pediatrics and Immunology; Academic, Researcher, Physician

"In this must-read book, Cindi not only exposes the hypocrisy of Corporate America, she points out how to move forward towards antiracism and accountability. This shift will be acutely painful in the short term for some, yet beneficial in the long term for everyone. Highly recommended for all who are trying to make a difference."

–Karen Fleshman, Esq., Founder, Racy Conversations

"Cindi Bright is one of the most powerful women I have the honor of calling a friend, colleague, and at times, co-catalyst. Her presence is the lightning that shakes your soul, and her words, the thunder that wakes your consciousness. A teacher, preacher, and prophet--this book will wake every person from their slumber and guide them towards truth and healing."

–Shirline Wilson, Washington State Director, Democrats for Education Reform

"Pour a glass of wine and prepare to be changed! Cindi's book is not only groundbreaking, but is an approachable tool for examining Corporate culture and gaining the discernment needed to be an advocate for BIPOC colleagues in the workplace. Courage is needed to unmask both the pressures and the people you will meet in your professional experiences. Cindi's compelling direction shows us the way."

–Dr. Tracy Williams, CEO Blue Squad Washington

THE COLOR OF
COURAGE

CRUSHING RACISM IN CORPORATE AMERICA

AVIVA
PUBLISHING
New York

CINDI BRIGHT

Published by:
Aviva Publishing
Lake Placid, NY
(518) 523-1320
www.AvivaPubs.com

Soft Cover ISBN: 978-1-63618-108-0
Hard Cover ISBN: 978-1-63618-036-6
eBook ISBN: 978-1-63618-137-0
Library of Congress Control Number: 2021900099

Editors: Erin Donley, Noelle Nightingale, Michael LaRocca
Cover & Interior Design: Fusion Creative Works, fusioncw.com

Every attempt has been made to properly source all quotes and attribute all research.

Printed in the United States of America
First Edition

From the cotton fields of
Jonesboro, Arkansas, to your first
grandson's Stanford education, this
book is dedicated to you, Dad.
You handed me the baton, and our
family's lineage has forever changed.

— Love, Cin

CONTENTS

FOREWORD
BY AARON BRIGHT

Can u c the pride in the pantha

as he glows in splendor and grace

Toppling OBSTACLES placed in the way

of the progression of his race

When my mom told me that she was going to write this book, I felt a roller coaster of emotions. I was excited but scared, proud but worried, inspired but fearful. Perhaps it's because my mom is an expert in a very sensitive subject (race relations). Or maybe it's because I've seen her scream explicit language towards a referee in a basketball game for calling a blocking foul on me when it was clear (in her view) that it was a charge on the other team. Oh, and it was just the first quarter!

Nevertheless, I knew writing this book was something my mom needed to do. I knew it wasn't about me. It was about her and our family's lineage.

Can u c the pride in the Pantha

as she nurtures her young all alone

The seed must grow regardless

of the fact that it's planted in stone

In 2015, the mega church Hillsong held a conference in New York City. At the time, I had just finished my collegiate basketball career, and pursuing my next venture felt like being an explorer without a compass. I was lost. Hoping to find inspiration and guidance, my mom and I bought tickets to the church's conference.

We watched several powerful sermons and sang to some of our favorite hymns in a stadium of 20,000+ people. But our favorite moment was the final sermon, when the last pastor hit the stage. His charisma was so emphatic, and his quick wit made it feel like, at times, you were at a comedy club. His name was Judah Smith.

We had seen Pastor Judah give countless Sunday services, as he was the Head Pastor for Churchome, based right in our backyard in Kirkland, Washington. But when I saw Pastor Judah perform in a stadium of thousands of people, I was mesmerized. "Wow," I thought. "People love him. Look at what he's built."

Funnily enough, when we returned home, Pastor Judah gave another sermon the next Sunday. His message caught me off guard. What was it, you ask? Well, it revolved around how the church and his family's "success" only exist because of the work of his dad--who co-founded the church. "We're all a product of our lineage," he said. "What you see today, the lights, the stage, the nice suits, the beautiful choir, doesn't exist without the work and sacrifices of those who came before me."

Can't u c the pride in the panthas

as they unify as one

The flower blooms with brilliance

and outshines the ray of the sun[1]

I can't tell you what's to come of the Bright family, but I can tell you that my mom's role in the trajectory of our lineage is as one that's anything but a bench player. Her impact will be felt for generations to come as the experiences and work she has done over the course of her life have built a foundation for our family that eventually will be felt by the masses.

What I ask of you is to not go into this book with the lens of reading the words of a crazy mom in the stands sending F Bombs to the ref. That's the "Ambitionz Az a Ridah" Cindi.[2]

I ask that you go into the book with the posture of reading the words of someone who stands for equality, equity, peace, and justice–the "Changes" Cindi.[3]

I am extremely proud of her and hope that you find her words inspiring and courageous. But most importantly--I hope that they spark action for the necessary change that is needed in all of us.

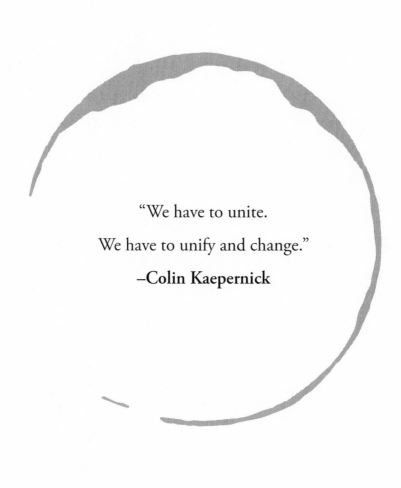

"We have to unite.

We have to unify and change."

–Colin Kaepernick

INTRODUCTION:
RAISE YOUR GLASSES

Dear Reader,

Before you begin, we need to talk. What you're about to en-counter is different from any leadership and business book you might have perused in the past. It's not meant to fill you with positivity or 10 steps to greater productivity. My goal is to disturb you to such a degree that the only satisfaction you'll find is to *do something* about the difficult things you've just read.

So let me pour you a glass of my favorite wine–Syrah.

If it were possible, I'd gather each and every one of you into a gorgeous winery in Napa Valley to sip this complex, dark-skinned, full-bodied creation. To me, this wine represents the lives of brown and Black individuals who have been harvested, fermented, pressed, and bottled by society.

And yet today, it's time for us to breathe, like a bottle of Syrah that's been freshly uncorked and poured into quality glassware.

You see, wine culture is my happy place. It's a space that allows me to think, relax, and even heal. In tasting rooms, I don't feel like an outsider. I feel deeply connected to people, nature, and even my faith. I want this experience for every brown and Black individual in America—to feel this sense of euphoria and cohesion not just in wineries, but everywhere. Brown and Black people deserve advocacy, and it goes beyond racial reconciliation. Everyone should be worthy of a great bottle of wine.

As a Corporate speaker and consultant, a former Human Resources executive, and a biracial person who is seen by the world as a Black woman, there's not a day when I don't witness or receive racism in business. It's built into every transaction and interaction, and has been normalized to a dangerous degree. Corporate America is a target of this book because it is a microcosm of America. What happens there plays out similarly in schools, communities, churches, nonprofits, and politics.

Brown and Black people are welcomed into corporations because we have the skills and ideas to make that company money. While profits from our contributions roll in, we find ourselves marginalized, discredited, and paid below our earning potential and our peers. If we try to hold people accountable or dare to fight for equality, Corporate will spare no expense to obliterate us. They've been unwilling to recognize the scars their precious workforce and racist practices have caused, which are spelled out in this book for you to understand.

Research from Echoing Green and Bridgespan says, "Race is one of the most reliable predictors of life outcomes across several areas, including life expectancy, academic achievement, income, wealth, physical and mental health, and maternal mortality. If socioeconomic difference explained these inequities, then controlling for socioeconomic status would eliminate them. But it does not."[1]

This statement explains why Corporate Racism is white America's problem to solve. White leaders in companies could put an end to our needless suffering, but it would take admitting there's a problem. That takes courage, first and foremost. Thankfully, there are lots of woke, white leaders stepping up to the plate. They realize that if they cannot identify the oppression at play, they won't be able to lead their teams into a place of inclusion. They won't be able to retain people of color in their organizations. They won't be considered a trusted person in the workplace, and most importantly, they will remain an everyday contributor to the degradation of brown and Black lives.

That's why I'm here, to teach you what Corporate white supremacy looks, sounds, and feels like, so you can identify when it's happening. White people have to gain discernment around this immediately. Brown and Black people are at the mercy of these organizations and systems that are destroying us. Just look at who's suffering most with COVID-19. It's brown and Black communities. That's why you see a revolution happening today, and it's why this book had to be written right now.

I was born in 1964, the tail end of the Baby Boomer generation. My Black father raised me to believe that I'd grow up, get a job, and work until retirement. He taught me to have a strong work ethic, along with "other" aspects of Corporate–the racial survival part. What he endured in the workplace was downright tragic. My head hurts and my shoulders ache, but I am determined not to pass on this mess to my son and my future grandchildren. This abusive cycle ends with me!

As a Corporate consultant, a mentor for Black women in business, a political/business talk show host, and now an author, I've had plenty of experience broaching racial topics. These aren't simple conversations. They require background information, foundational knowledge, and clear ideas about how to move forward. That's why I've laid out this book in an intentional manner for you.

In chapter one, you'll hear my personal story of climbing the Corporate ladder. It began with raw ambition and naivete, and ended in a nasty court case against my employer that affected my health, wealth, and career for many years. As you might expect, names have been changed to protect people's privacy, but it's important for you to see how it all went down. Who hurt me the most is not who you might expect.

In chapter two, I tease out my interactions with the players in my story, so you can better see the manipulative nature of oppression at work. This chapter also explains the fixed set of rules in Corporate that Good Ole Boys culture enforces without apology. No doubt, you'll see traits of this toxic environment reflected in your coworkers, boss, vendors, and even shareholders. The point is to recognize how this looks in your world.

In chapter three, we step back from critiques to help you distinguish the grossly unhelpful responses to racial accusations. This means you'll need to uncover the oppressive thoughts that have been programmed into your head. No one is exempt. This chapter will also help you seek out bigotry in your surroundings to minimize difficulty for all marginalized groups of people. These abusers need to be taken down now!

In chapter four, we dive into a delicate topic—white women's harm. Growing up, I had a challenging relationship with my white mom. She showed me how white women who haven't healed their own issues can cause a world of hurt to other women. This chapter dissects women's leadership and will teach you to distinguish which women are worthy of having power over people's lives. This chapter was the toughest for me to write, though essential to your learning.

In chapter five, I name the gatekeepers that keep brown and Black folx from gaining wealth and power in Corporate. You also get to learn what Corporate practices are disguised as being good, yet are a facade for further racism. My ideas for transformation aren't simple. They'll make a lot of people mad, but they are starting points to greater peace and racial progress.

In chapter six, I speak directly to brown and Black professionals, and offer final inspiration to white anti-racism leaders.

My journey has taken many twists and turns. In 2018, I ran for public office in my city of Bellevue, Washington–hellbent on changing outcomes and policies for Black and brown people. It was a grueling 90-hour per week undertaking that was practically impossible as a single, Black woman. I lost the election, but gained a wider perspective of racism, sexism, and all forms of oppression in society. Since then, race relations has become an obsessive topic for me. I can sniff it out anywhere I go and describe it with precision.

In my work with large Corporate clients and mid-size businesses, company leaders appreciate my pro-business stance, my ability to speak their language, and my speed in being able to pinpoint their racial inequities. We don't have to go slow or dance around topics. They trust me to give it to them straight. I demonstrate that same directness each week on my program, HeartBeat radio. For the last three years, I've interviewed hundreds of leaders in a variety of industries, community positions, and politics, and I've always touched upon topics that people generally want to avoid because they're controversial, yet crucial to address for racial freedom.

My life hasn't been smooth. Like many people of color, I have had trauma, abuse, fear, and searing betrayals to heal. Working on myself has kept my courage and stamina strong. And at the end of the day, it's still my reflection in the mirror that I'm learning to love unconditionally. My prayer is always to help me learn further discernment, wisdom, and knowledge, so that I can grow in this process too.

Something powerful happens when you align with your purpose. My determination has been set aflame, and I've been given a vision for change—one that liberates brown and Black people from bondage and holds the oppressors accountable. They will not win. This, I know with every fiber in my being.

So again, please join me in having a delicious glass of Syrah. Even if you don't drink alcohol, you can still appreciate the path this dark-skinned varietal has taken from vine to glass. Brown and Black folx in Corporate America have been similarly harvested, fermented, pressed, and bottled. It's interesting with wine–grapes that struggle most on the vine are the ones that need the most air. Today, it's time for people of color to breathe freely.

Raise your glasses for a toast:

> *May we learn to face our demons, respect all human life, and find courage to crush racism in our communities and Corporate spaces. This monumental endeavor will take every one of us, and every ounce of discomfort will be worth it. That, I can promise you.*

Cheers to your efforts,
Cindi

"God will break you into position
He will break you to promote you
And break you to put you in your right place
But when He breaks you He doesn't hurt you,
When He breaks you, He doesn't destroy you.
He does it with; grace"

—Tasha Cobbs Leonard, "Gracefully Broken"

1

MY STORY OF
WORKPLACE RACISM

Karen didn't tell me right away about the affair. I started to observe something different in her behavior. Despite having natural confidence, there was a noticeable spring in her step. Karen was a petite, smart, pretty, blonde, white woman. Those five traits often pave a smooth road for women in Corporate America, but Karen's smile insinuated that something was up her sleeve. I knew she'd tell me eventually.

Hired as Human Resource execs on the exact same day, our friendship quickly blossomed. Almost instantly, we realized we had walked into a shit storm together. Although quite reputable, Financial Services Inc. had minimal processes and infrastructure to move the business forward. Karen and I had comparable career experience and equal fierceness. United, our tasks ahead didn't seem as daunting.

My love for fine wine was developing at this time, and through my learning and appreciation, I started teaching Karen. Soon, we were gathering on weekends to share delicious bottles of vino and uncork from pressures at work. So I remember inquiring about what was going on with her. We were sitting in my backyard over the firepit talking about our troubles. That's when she confessed to having an affair with Ken, the CFO of the company.

I gasped. "Karen, you can't be the HR director and be sleeping with the CFO. That's a conflict of interest." My goal wasn't to scold her. I just saw all the ways this could be disastrous. She was sleeping with someone who had power over her and others in the company. Plus, she was in charge of people's jobs and had private information on them. "You can't let that slip during pillow talk. People are supposed to come to us in confidence," I pleaded. I felt scared for the mountain of challenges she (and the company) could face if this ever became public. Mostly, I just felt afraid for my friend who was stuck in a toxic relationship.

At this point, Karen was no longer drunk in love. Their honeymoon phase had included lavish meals, blatant PDA, and trips to romantic places, but she'd been increasingly unhappy with him, and for good reason. Get this—he was asking her to pay for everything. Karen often complained about her credit card bill. Later I learned he was avoiding any records of their affair. He even had the audacity to use our company credit cards for a few of their dinners, so he was taking advantage of the company too. Regardless, Karen decided to leave her husband to be with the still-married CFO as much as he would see her.

A myriad of complaints started coming through on the company ethics hotline. Not just casual complaints, but pointed ones. By now, Karen had rented an apartment across the street from the office, which sent signals ablaze. Ken and Karen were literally having sex at lunchtime a few hundred feet away from the office. I could never prove it, but I suspect Ken's assistant stirred up rumors. The hotline comments offered specifics only someone with access to C-Suite schedules could have known.

Karen wasn't scared or embarrassed, but rather angry. She wanted the assistant to be fired. I coached her not to push that envelope because it could be construed as retaliation. I also feared that Karen could get caught in a scandal. Having been privy to hidden information about the finances of the company, she knew a few things that could get her in trouble. I begged her to leave him, but above all, I encouraged Karen to talk to Sue, our global HR boss. "Tell her you need a transfer!" It was imperative for Karen to get out of the reporting relationship she had with Ken. That would take away the perception of impropriety.

My mind raced over this situation because frankly, Karen's poor decisions reminded me of my own. I had my share of men challenges in the past and could relate to her struggles. Regardless, tensions grew between Karen and me. No matter how much I showed up as her friend, she viewed my angst as a rejection of her. Admittedly, I was struggling to find words for my emotions. I just kept telling her, "Shit's about to explode!"

Because of my position in HR, I was asked to look into hotline complaints. I did my due diligence and eventually had no choice but to tell our boss, Sue, whose conclusion was thankfully in line with mine. We needed to make damn sure the company didn't come down on Karen only. After all, she wasn't in the position of power like Ken. Sue went straight to John, the CEO, to discuss the matter. We both had a good relationship with him and trusted he would handle this reasonably.

Soon after, I found out Sue had been fired along with Dimitri, the Head of Compensation, my friend and peer. My adrenaline kicked into gear as I grabbed the phone to call Sue. When she picked up, she was rattled and unable to be open about what was going down. I knew she was capable of taking good care of herself. Sue was smart like that. As you can imagine, the buzz around the office was deafening. No one could understand why Sue and Dimitri had been fired. I, however, had a sneaking suspicion of what had quietly transpired.

That night, while I was trying to wrap my head around derivatives in class (pursuing my MBA), a text arrived from one of my teammates. They said an announcement had just come out about my decision to leave the company. Wait, my decision to do what? The termination letter Financial Services Inc. gave me the next day was worded differently: "We are exercising our right as an at-will employer."

You don't say these words to a Black HR woman and expect her not to understand what's really being said. In veiled "legal language" they told me, "We have no justification to fire you, but we are going to do it anyways." My fear had come true. I knew this was just the beginning of a horrific situation ahead.

You'd think Ken and Karen would be fired next, right? Nope, Ken never lost his job. And Karen? I saw that she eventually left and walked away with a healthy severance, as did Sue and Dimitri. As for me? I got nothing, only a vague letter to say I was fired for no reason, at least not one they could name quite yet.

When I made some noise and threatened with charges of discrimination and wrongful termination, I thought it would provoke their sense of reasoning. It wound up back-firing on me. They flat out refused to settle. For the next 18 months, Financial Services Inc. prepared to take me down financially, mentally, professionally, and emotionally in a court of law, a task they could not even tackle without the help of one white woman—Karen. And so the unraveling of my life began in a substantial way.

Let me give you some backstory.

I started at Financial Services Inc. in November 2012 and was thrilled to work at this prestigious firm with a strong reputation. Karen and I were hired by Sue, the global head of Human Resources. We were based in Seattle, Washington, while Sue was housed in the New York City office. Financial Services Inc. had been recruiting me for quite a while, but I kept turning them down because, well, the world is small. Their interim HR Director was a notorious asshole I knew from another company.

During the recruitment process, a white woman from Financial Services Inc. named Becky had been heavily courting me. Everyone knows executives get brownie points for bringing on a diversity hire. It felt like Becky's sincerity was performative and her enthusiasm was forced. I wasn't going to be claimed as her token hire. My priority was to know if I'd have a boss that I could confide in if shit ever hit the fan.

At this point in my career, I knew better than to leap without investigating. Would I respect Sue as my boss? Would she respect me? How many other "Beckys" circled the halls of Financial Services Inc.? That's why I insisted on meeting Sue in person. They kept telling me, "Well, she's based in New York." And I kept responding, "Well, I'm happy to fly there." I had to make sure I could actually work for this woman.

Up to this point, I had mostly worked for men and was pretty intentional about that. White women have been my biggest tormentors, as they are for many people of color. Men have always been much kinder and supportive to me than white women. I noticed this as a kid and had this truth validated repeatedly throughout my career.

Another reason for wanting to meet Sue was to understand if Financial Services Inc. was in fact honoring the job description they had posted. Their ad said they were looking for "progressive" business people. My progressive outlook is that people are the greatest assets of a business. They're also the biggest pain points, mostly because companies treat them poorly. My progressive goals focused on these challenging, people-focused issues. Did their idea of progressive match mine, or did they ultimately want an HR person to push through piles of paperwork? These were my burning questions.

And so Sue flew to a nearby Financial Services Inc. office, and I drove about an hour to meet her. We spent just 30 minutes together, and before I had arrived back home, they had offered me the job. I happily accepted. Needless to say, Sue and I connected instantly. She was a brilliant, no-nonsense, British woman who allowed me to relax and be proud to have this lucrative, game-changing opportunity.

Sue was brought into the company to turn it around after the financial crisis of 2008. Financial Services Inc. was exposed for doing a poor job of diversifying portfolios. In turn, they took a big hit, which prompted the hiring of John, the new CEO tasked with the company's return to profitability. John chose Sue, perhaps because she had incredible discernment and delivery. I mean, her communication skills were downright exceptional, and she was respected for it. Sue was forward thinking, academic, and her strong U.K. accent cut through the noise of a boardroom. That's no small feat, mind you. Financial Services Inc. was the textbook definition of Good Ole Boys culture at the time.

I was hired to run Human Resources for three of the company's business lines. One of them, the Indexes business, was their most profitable business. Another was the mutual funds business, referred to as Private Client Services. The third was a new venture for Financial Services Inc., an Exchange Trade Funds business based in the Bay Area and NYC. As the head of HR, I was involved in building and growing that business from the ground up. This gives you some perspective on the acumen I was gaining and the responsibility that fell on my shoulders.

Early on, I didn't know anything about financial services, let alone how money was made. The learning curve was steep, and I was thankful to Sue and three CEOs with whom I had reporting relationships. They were wonderful to me. Within no time, I was off and running. Then in my 40s with a college-aged son, I had more freedom to travel to our San Francisco and NYC offices. As I zipped coast-to-coast for business, I came to appreciate what it felt like to be an executive and a person of influence.

Our business leaders respected me and saw that I had strong business intuition. They acknowledged my thirst to learn, valued my focus on people, and applauded my no-nonsense approach to productivity. Perhaps the best compliment was, they never questioned my dedication to help them succeed. I cared about them immensely and spent off-hours with them and their families. We shared exquisite meals and yes, drank tons of fabulous wine. I had finally elevated into a role where I could rise and thrive.

One of my favorite memories at Financial Services Inc. happened in New York City. My colleagues accompanied me to my son's championship game at Madison Square Garden. Aaron was studying at Stanford University and had just been named MVP of the NIT, National Invitation Tournament. Earlier, we all spent time at Wall Street ringing the bell over our new fund that had just launched. Dinner at Il Mulino followed, simply a jaw-dropping, top-notch restaurant.

The Chief Legal Officer was sitting next to me at the table. He whispered, "Don't tell anyone what I just ordered," as he requested a few bottles of ridiculously expensive wine. We chuckled and I said, "I'm not biting off the hand that feeds me." It was such a spectacular evening. As the only woman at a table of successful white men, I felt alive, like I had arrived and belonged. They genuinely liked me.

I mean, what's not to like? I solved problems for them and took bullets for these guys. I did a lot of their dirty work, as we in Human Resources get paid to do. But I also made a point to look out for people, ensuring they were treated fairly. I rectified pay issues, and not just for marginalized groups, but for anyone who wasn't being adequately compensated. I was really good at this job and embraced it wholeheartedly. Yep, that little Black girl who had been to hell and back was making strides at a major financial services company.

Like anything, there were downsides. Becky, the woman from the hiring process, was head of the company's service center. Her view of HR was very old school, traditional. Her team members were "rule following" people. It was probably one of their first jobs where they had a little bit of power, and it showed. They were minions who saluted the boss and enforced an autocratic style of managing. I have no hesitation in calling these people downright horrible.

So I refused to let Becky, who sorely lacked business foresight, project her 1950s-era process onto my businesses. I told her, "This company should not be paying someone like me to fill out forms." I worked for the most profitable businesses at Financial Services Inc., and she expected me to do administrative work that was not in my skill set. I was a leader. I had vision. Yet I had to constantly argue that I wasn't brought in to be an admin.

It went beyond that. There wasn't a day when Becky's minions wouldn't push back on my simple requests. They would refuse to run reports for me and say, "Do it yourself." It was as though they'd rather die than become an extension of my success. Becky provided zero help in resolving these issues. In fact, she fanned the flames.

The HR and business department women also ran a powerful gossip ring. I had to set up meetings with them to confront rumors about me and the CEO sleeping together. They knew Rob and I had a great relationship. The office space had all glass doors and conference rooms, so everyone could see into the rooms. Even still, these women gained their self-esteem by stirring up trouble for me. They couldn't accept that my success occurred without screwing someone to get there.

In reality, what these HR women were seeing was the genuine connection I had with Rob. We trusted each other. I fought tooth and nail to get him higher portions of bonus pools and was successful in helping him grow the company's bottom line, which put tons of cash in his pocket. I also protected his reputation. Rob was a drinker and partier, but not in a negative way. In financial services, it's common and somewhat expected to entertain and engage in this consistent and sometimes excessive fashion.

Enduring the backhanded comments about my working relationship with Rob was ongoing and tiring. I asked these women if they understood how destructive they were being. Rob was married and his family could have been torn apart. As a leader in the company, I expected Becky to squash these nasty rumors amongst her team, but I sensed they actually brought her joy to see me uncomfortable.

In my years at Financial Services Inc., Becky desperately tried to marginalize not just me, but Karen too. She didn't like Sue either. The impression we all had was that Becky had to be the smartest woman in the room. Anyone who presented themselves with confidence, clarity, and determination would be deemed a threat to her. Karen would pander to Becky's need for superiority, then bitch behind her back. That always drove me crazy. On the flip side, I kept meeting Becky toe-to-toe to instigate and insist on change.

By this point, I'd had enough of these toxic HR people and wanted to be around business-minded folks. Financial Services Inc. saw me as a high performer, and I envisioned my transition into a general manager-type of position. That's why they agreed to pay for me to get my MBA. Turns out, I didn't have to wait until graduation to get some reprieve. Sue had been tracking Becky's deceptive antics and poor leadership style. For these reasons and more, Sue eventually fired her.

By this time, Karen and I had worked tirelessly to implement new systems. This bonded us both professionally and personally. Like many women, Karen had trauma in her past. This led to conversations that were intensely private between us–conversations that required the utmost trust, which we gave to each other. At one point, Karen confided in me about the CFO's unhealthy patterns and tendencies. Hearing that nearly killed me, so I invited Karen to stay with me until she could untangle from this man. As her friend and fellow woman, I just wanted her to break free.

When the news hit that Sue had been suddenly fired, Karen and I got together for lunch. Our friendship took a nosedive that day. All along, I had been explaining to Karen why we needed Sue and how much we could trust her. "She'll be on your side," I promised. But with Sue now gone, it was too late. Karen knew that I had shared her secret with Sue, and I realized within minutes, there was nothing I could say to help.

Karen wouldn't acknowledge my duty in HR to report back to Sue, nor would she take responsibility for her part. She viewed this as my attempt to ruin her life. And you know what? The more irate she became at me, the more in love she became with the CFO.

At that final lunch together, I'll never forget Karen staring directly into my eyes. The room got cold as she muttered, "You just wait, Cindi Bright. You just wait." Chills ran through my body because I knew based on my history with white women that even if she were my friend, she could turn like a light switch, which is exactly what she did.

With Karen, I had been sharing my revelations from therapy, or I'd share the surprises in my day. For instance, I had a one-time fling with Dimitri, our Head of Compensation—yep, the guy that was fired right after Sue. It was a spontaneous occurrence after a work party in New York. It was consensual, and he was my peer, not my superior. So technically, it wasn't an abuse of power or against company protocol. I told my friend about that one night with Dimitri and trusted she'd keep it safe.

Karen took everything she knew about me and shared it with company lawyers to build their case. She exposed and embellished aspects of my life that were deeply painful, along with the traumas and abuses I'd endured. Additionally, Karen and Becky hired the same lawyer to protect themselves to double up their ammo to destroy my life and career.

With Sue's position now vacant, Financial Services Inc. filled it with one of my HR peers from Canada, a white woman named Carol. Carol used to come into town, and I'd be the one to meet her at the hotel and take her to dinner. Now, we all have people we can't stand at work, but Carol had been high on my list. I had to bite my tongue so many times with this woman. From experiences with her, I'd label her a racist, hands down. But I took the high road with her, which was to be inclusive and make her feel welcomed. What other choice did I have?

Now in the position of global HR director, one of Carol's jobs was to help the company obliterate me in court. It was no surprise that she willingly obliged. So Carol repeatedly traveled to Seattle, ready to be a foot soldier of the patriarchy. How?

Well, for one, she agreed to take Sue's job for about one fifth of the salary Sue had made. Carol didn't care what this position was worth on the market, nor did she care about her own financial worth. Instead she chose to wield (temporary) power. That's the funny part. Carol was actually fired too. She was hired as a hit man to cheaply work on my case, while also fulfilling Sue's old duties. When the trial was complete, they kicked Carol to the curb. She worked for pennies, compared to what she could have earned, just to take down another woman. When her task was complete, they booted her.

Preparing for the trial was the most difficult task I've ever undertaken. Just months before graduation, I would leave school at 4 pm and head to my attorney's office to review our discovery materials. Judith was a seasoned, badass, civil rights attorney. Then in her 70s, she was a pro at her job and was patient in helping me prepare. This included reviewing thousands of pages of emails, texts, and instant messages from a myriad of people at Financial Services Inc.

While reading what people said about each other and me, I began to feel ill. It was a shock to realize these people would smile in the hallways, then say awful things behind my back. I saw women talk about other women in the most disparaging ways. I saw tons of affairs that no one knew about. My texts were visible to them too, and I wasn't proud of some of the foul language I had used. There was a big mirror held up for me to examine myself. It didn't feel good, but it sure was needed. One cannot go through public embarrassment and discreditment and go back to the normalcy of life again. It changed my behavior and conjured profound personal growth.

The trial began in June 2014, just 10 days after my graduation. Judith and I tried everything to settle out of court, but they insisted on dragging me through a four-week emotional roller coaster. Their primary motive was to put my mental health on display and paint it as undoubtedly damaged. They subpoenaed my therapist, wanting to see their records and notes. Yeah, you read that right. Everything you think is confidential at a therapist's office can be used against you. I always felt paranoid when my longtime therapist would start scrolling on the page. Something inside me knew those words weren't safe with them.

Financial Services Inc. researched every aspect of my life until age 50 and presented a narrative that was exaggerated, untrue, and hurtful, yet also painfully humbling. They put me on display and told everyone that I was psychotic, promiscuous, and deeply troubled—an incompetent Black woman who used the race card to get everything she wants in life. They even used the term "Malingerer" to describe me. That is what they called slaves who faked sickness.

Pre-trial, I was required to meet with a "health expert" that Financial Services Inc. hired to offer his assessment of my mental wellbeing. After two hours, he summarized my 50 years of life and testified that termination of my employment was justified. They paid this doctor something like $60,000 for his damaging testimony.

I was asked recently if the health expert might have revealed some valid concerns. I told them every Black woman has trauma. The daily news alone is traumatizing for us. To see your sons, daughters, aunties, uncles, friends, partners, and parents get terrorized and murdered by police is enough to traumatize anyone. You don't make it to adulthood as a Black person in America without being triggered by the racism all around you. That's what I worked on with my therapist, which actually indicates my mental strength, not weakness.

As expected, their attorney brought up a fling with the Head of Compensation. But they didn't just say it was in-appropriate, they accused me of trading sexual favors for compensation information. As a head of HR, I already had access to compensation information. Their attorney was this little, weaselly-eyed, white boy. I said to him, "Do you realize what you just said? You just called me a whore in open court." My head turned to the judge. With my heart rate pulsing, I exclaimed, "I need a break!" That moment sent me over the top.

During time-out, the judge called the counsel up to the bench. He told them to cool it with the name calling. When we resumed, I assumed they'd move on, having been chastised by the judge. Nope. They fell right back into the same storyline of me whoring myself for information to help marginalized folks gain unfair advantages.

The defense claimed I had abused my authority by giving people compensation they were unworthy to receive. To back them up, they brought a white woman manager named Sharon onto the stand. For months, Sharon had been squawking to me about a Black man on her team. She did not think he deserved the $30,000 increase that Rob, Ken, and I had approved for him. This man was brilliant and a gigantic asset to our company. We didn't give him an unfair wage, we fixed the pay gap between him and his teammates. Sharon found that to be unacceptable and made sure that was known. That's one reason she seemed elated to get on the stand against me. The irony is—months earlier, I was the one who went to bat to fix the income gap for Sharon's pay. Did she not recall? All I could do was shake my head at her ungratefulness and entitlement as she gleefully tried to discredit me.

Their final argument against me was to imply that my passion for quality wine wasn't just a hobby, but an addiction. I had always been the social HR person who would go wine tasting and have cocktails with colleagues. Some of our best times as a team were spent over delicious dinners and decadent wine. That's common for Corporate culture. So I was part of the group then, but when they needed to gain power in their defense, they labeled me a drunk. How convenient.

There were moments in the trial when my attorney would look at me and say, "I got you." She wasn't going to let me be a lone warrior. I had been so used to fighting for myself. Watching her take the floor, work the room, and catch the defense in their lies brought me endless comfort. She had two lawyers on the bench with her and the confidence of all three of them combined. I couldn't have endured the company's smear campaign without Judith's support and unconditional love.

Of the 13 jurors, most of them were white, and strangely enough, three were HR people. I remember telling Judith that I didn't want those damn HR people on my jury. I envisioned Becky's gossip hounds getting off by punishing a Black woman. But truth be told, it was the HR gals who tipped the jury in my favor because they understood the laws.

Yep, I won the trial. It was the second largest employment related discrimination lawsuit in the state of Washington.

The jury awarded me back pay and my annual wage, and because I had just secured my MBA, they figured I could head back to Corporate and instantly make more money with my advanced degree. Ugh, are you kidding? Why would I subject myself to that environment again?

Even though I won the case, my award didn't sustain me for long. There was no forward thinking by the jurors about the trauma this whole ordeal had caused and the healing that would be needed. If this verdict had come down today, I would have been given enough money to relax and retire.

It's been nearly a decade, and the pain is still palpable. I still cry a lot. It's difficult to pick yourself back up at 50 years old, after your stability, self-worth, and ability to trust have been shattered. I've gone without food for a few days when I had no money. I've slept in my car, crashed on people's couches, and stayed with someone who made me feel like I was in prison. I've also remained single and have been worn down by having no partner to depend on–at least in physical form.

I battled breast cancer recently too. One could argue that decades of stress on my body were a huge contributor to my weak immune system. It often felt like I had no reason to live. Tears stream as I write this, remembering the isolation and suffering that was caused by Karen's need for power, protection, retaliation, money, and the love of a man. She could have joined forces with her sisters, Sue and me. Instead she launched an expensive, time consuming trial designed to destroy my future and save hers.

In the next chapter, we're going to examine Good Ole Boys culture in Corporate. Now that you know my story, you'll be able to follow my references to characters like Karen, Rob, Carol, and Becky. You'll also have context for the Corporate culture in which I soared until I became a threat to the white powers that be.

"With secrets you can't tell
Mix a special brew
Put fire inside of you
But anytime you feel
Danger or Fear
Instantly, I will appear"

–Chaka Khan, "I'm Every Woman"

2

10 COMMANDMENTS OF THE GOB

In this chapter, I'm going to tease out my interactions with Karen, Becky, and Carol, as well as the men at Financial Services Inc., so you can see the normalized and manipulative nature of oppression in the workplace. The goal of this chapter is to see yourself, your boss, coworkers, shareholders, vendors, and clients in my story. Karen and the crew were not evil exceptions. They are no different from your average white person in Corporate who has been groomed to win at all costs.

Let's go back to my story and look at how white supremacy has been accepted in Corporate and how you can better spot it. It starts by understanding the foundation rules of that environment. Arab gender researcher and poet Farida D. nails this explanation:

"Not all white people uphold white supremacy;
But white supremacy upholds all white people.

Not all cis men uphold patriarchy;
but patriarchy upholds all cis men.

Not all heterosexuals uphold heteronormativity;
but heteronormativity upholds all heterosexuals.

Not all able-bodies uphold ableism;
but ableism upholds all able-bodies.

Not all the rich uphold classism;
but classism upholds all the rich.

Not all the privileged uphold systems of oppression;
but systems of oppression are upheld by the silence of
those it privileges."[1]

10 COMMANDMENTS OF THE GOB

For decades, Corporate America has been steeped in Good
Ole Boys culture. What does that mean? We could refer
to this oppressive system as the Patriarchy, but that causes
people to think it's only about men. We could also name it
white supremacy, but that causes people to think it's only
about race. For the sake of brevity, I'll refer to Good Ole
Boys culture as the GOB, but please know, this hierarchical
force feeds all the "isms"–racism, sexism, homophobia, ableism, transphobia, ageism, etc.

The GOB ultimately serves white men in positions of power, yet it would not and could not survive without white women keeping this cruelty in place. If women got on the same page about what was unacceptable, we would literally topple the patriarchy overnight. That's why it's imperative to know the rules of the GOB, namely how it habitually defends and protects itself.

To help you understand, I've compiled 10 principles that are used to serve the GOB's interests. They're called commandments because the powers that be in Corporate follow them religiously.

1. PROTECT THY WHITE MAN

The hierarchy in Corporate (and everywhere) places the white man firmly at the top. If a man holds power in the company or community, he will have free reign to break rules and dominate anyone who holds less power. It doesn't matter who is affected by the words and actions of prominent white men, they will always be protected, first and foremost.

When looking back on my story, doesn't it amaze you that the CFO never lost his job? There were no professional consequences for Ken, a company executive, who had dated a subordinate, misused company credit cards, sparked office-wide disruption, and prompted the firing of Sue, Dimitri, and me. The destructive actions of a white man truly don't matter. They are shielded with a fierce army of brainwashed, power-hungry people who believe they're doing the right thing. Newsflash: They're actually doing the *white* thing!

White women are groomed to protect their men. Just look at how Karen safeguarded Ken at the expense of Sue and me. Even though we made her the priority when the affair exploded, she rejected our loyalty and chose him instead. Even though he asked her to pay for everything and showed unhealthy tendencies, she chose him again over her own safety and sanity. This is a prime example of how women are used and manipulated by the GOB. Their aim to 'protect thy white man' puts them and their sisters directly in harm's way.

White women literally co-sign their own oppression by agreeing to protect thy white man. They still aren't getting equal pay, they're not immune to sexism and abuse, and their worth in GOB culture is often determined by what kind of dirty work they're willing to do. Carol demonstrated this when she accepted a position for a fifth of the income she should have received. She sacrificed hundreds of thousands of dollars for herself to ultimately protect thy white man!

When Rob, the CEO, got on the witness stand against me during the trial, my heart fell into my stomach. Our infinite laughs, riveting conversations, and shared success were erased that day. All it took was one of his buddies getting busted, and all bets were off with me. Same was true with other colleagues who testified against me. They saw with their own two eyes the bullshit that was happening. In the end, they chose to 'protect thy white man.' Why? Because they want proximity to power, which you cannot get when you align with the marginalized.

'Protect thy white man' is the first commandment for a reason. It sets the stage for all the others and has a damaging effect for brown and Black professionals.

2. REJECT TRUTH AND ACCOUNTABILITY

Imagine if Ken, the CFO, would have come clean and said, "Listen, everyone, I am at fault here. I disobeyed my role as a leader and deserve to be fired. Please keep going without me." Do you realize how much time, money, and energy would have been saved if truth and accountability would have been acknowledged upfront? That isn't possible though because honesty is kryptonite for the GOB. Denial is their superpower, and lying is essential to their strength. Cover-ups used by Financial Services Inc.:

- They lied in the all-staff email about their reason for firing me.

- They claimed I had unfairly compensated people of color.

- They said I "whored myself" to get compensation information.

- They fabricated my mental instability and alcohol addiction.

- They said I played the 'race card' to gain advantages.

White men aren't the only benefactors of this second GOB Commandment. Remember, Karen refused accountability and demanded the removal of Sue and me, as well as threatening Ken's assistant. She could dodge truth and accountability because she was aligned with those in power.

Carol exhibited Corporate's rejection of truth when on the witness stand, she claimed they were going to keep me employed, despite my romp with Dimitri, until I spoke openly about the double standards at play. You see, I wasn't shy about asking, "Why are the CFO and HR Director allowed to be free of punishment, while Dimitri and I have warranted an investigation?" We were peers! There's no rule against employees having sex. But truth was not allowed to be spoken there. Essentially, they wanted me to move on as if nothing had occurred. As long as the Black woman shuts up and bows down, they'll keep us employed. If we defend ourselves or try to speak honestly, they'll take us down. Reject truth and accountability—the GOB and its supporters are actually quite skilled at this.

The most obvious example of this second commandment is NFL quarterback Colin Kaepernick, who quietly kneeled during the National Anthem to honor Black lives harmed by police brutality. He was met with rage from players, fans, coaches, and the white male team owners. Jerry Jones of the Dallas Cowboys threatened punishment for players who joined Kaepernick in taking a knee. He said he would bench players for disrespecting the flag.[2] This slave/master mentality conveyed a clear message to his Black players. Essentially, he said, "You can make me millions of dollars, but don't you dare stand for your truth, and don't you dare expect us to honor or believe you."

You might be wondering why truth cannot be accepted by the GOB. It's not as complex as you might think. Truth must be rejected because it could compromise their wealth and families, it would require them to acknowledge the harm they've caused, and it would end the advantages given to white people in power. That's a hassle they're not willing to deal with, nor is it required so they choose to destroy brown and Black lives instead.

3. ENFORCE RACIAL STEREOTYPES

Racist labels for Black women include angry, vengeful, calculating, psychotic, promiscuous, and addicted. These accusations have been hurled at *all* women for centuries, and they're still used today to paint a picture of incapability, particularly for Black women. The GOB is adept at weaponizing racial stereotypes. It's yet another tactic to protect white men and to reject truth and accountability.

I've heard my entire career things like, "You know, Cindi, you have such a strong presence. You can be really intimidating." They've said I was arrogant and full of myself. As a Black woman, I've had to work hard not to come across as mad or overpowering. This is no easy feat. It's not that I am pissed off all the time, it's just that I'm required in business to keep up a smile, laugh when offended, hold back my views, and build relationships with people I cannot stand. All of this to avoid these ridiculous assumptions applied to all Black women. Even then, it doesn't always work!

Because these pervasive stereotypes persist, brown and Black professionals have learned how to code switch to survive in the workplace. This is the practice of shifting our natural speech to match what white people can handle. We have to walk on eggshells the entire time at work. We have to choose our battles carefully. We can't afford to let our true selves show because that's when the attacks start. It's a 'damned if you do, damned if you don't' situation because one insecure white person can ruin your whole life at any point. You just never know.

Case in point—when tensions rose between Karen and me, she could not see my genuine concern for her. She could not remember our deep bonds as friends. She could only see me as malicious and "beneath her." My childhood experience at school was similar. I was teased and mocked for being mixed race, having different hair, being poor, and wearing hand-me-downs. No one was interested in knowing the real me or seeing my value as a person. My mom once bought me what I thought was a stylish pair of red pointy shoes at Goodwill. I was elated to have cute girl shoes, but was ridiculed by my classmates. Repeatedly.

One day in middle school, I got jumped by a white girl and was summoned to the principal's office. When I told the principal what happened, the white girl denied it, and he believed her. I learned a valuable lesson that day—when a white woman defends herself, even through lies, her words are the gospel. But when a Black woman speaks up for herself, she is labeled the problem. That still rings true today. It was painful to be seen as untrustworthy, problematic, and not worth protecting in the eyes of adults. Imagine what that does to a little person's confidence and nervous system, and to their sense of safety and reality as they develop into adulthood. When this behavior goes on every single day of the year, we develop a deeper sense of "being attacked" because we are always looking over our shoulders.

White people, but especially white women, habitually assume the worst about Black women, and people believe them. And if the white person's criticism isn't compelling enough, the GOB will pull strings to prove they are right. This deflects from the real issues created by white people in the workplace and explains why the oppressed get put on trial. Financial Services Inc. paid a mental health expert

$60K to testify that my stability was in question. In reality, my mental health had nothing to do with getting fired without severance, and it had nothing to do with Karen and Ken's affair.

Do you also recall the HR department gossiping about me having an affair with Rob the CEO, and how the defense claimed I had slept with Dimitri to obtain compensation information? You see, any time Black women have business relationships with men, it's assumed we're using sex to get what we want. Our work ethic and results aren't enough proof for the GOB. They need to believe we are calculating, promiscuous, and cannot be trusted.

Why? Because it makes them feel better about protecting the white man. That's how they sleep at night after rejecting truth and accountability. Enforcing racial stereotypes is a tried and true practice for GOB culture and for the advancement of white supremacy. All the while, brown and Black people struggle to gain health, wealth, and status.

The hypocrisy of the GOB is worthy of marveling. Remember how they called me a whore in court for sleeping with Dimitri? Why was that label not given to Karen? She was married, I was not. Why wasn't Ken condemned either? He was married too.

Here's how it goes—when a Black woman has sex with anyone but her partner, she is a whore. But white boys swinging dicks? That's normal. And the white woman boinking the high powered CFO? Well, she can't help how she feels, now can she? Let's not judge or interrupt their love.

Obviously, Black women aren't the only ones impacted by racial bias. All of us brown and Black people will likely be deemed "performance problems" in Corporate America. This is a gigantic failure of the system to understand people's history and trauma. It's also a way to skirt accountability for the oppressors. We'll dig into that more in upcoming chapters. For now, let's keep going with the GOB Commandments.

4. REWARD THY PLEASERS

When Karen spilled my secrets and past traumas, she gave the company everything they needed to deny discrimination and claim innocence in my firing. The dirt she gave them about my private life protected her from getting punished for her role in the affair. That's what happens when you please the GOB. White women know how this works. 'Reward thy pleasers' ensures that the white man is protected, the truth gets buried, and brown and Black folx can be discriminated against at any time. It also ensures the pleaser gets what *they* want too.

What does it mean to be a pleaser? Pleasers are insincere and have an agenda. Think of a teenager trying to gain access to their parents' car. "Mom, have I mentioned how beautiful you look today? Can I help you clean out the garage this weekend?" There's a hidden motive. Corporate pleasers are no different. They also pride themselves on being rule followers, as Becky's team demonstrated. Their role of enforcer was like it was a badge of honor for them. It made them believe they were good white women. Pleasers know that if they can provide secret information, compliment the right people, or alert the staff of anything peculiar, they will be included, they'll be trusted, they will gain in title, income, or social power.

For years, people didn't believe I was Black when they spoke to me on the phone. They'd say, "Oh, my gosh. You sound white!" That's because I've had to soften my tone and sugar coat my words to get as far as I have. This isn't being fake, it's being a survivalist in Corporate America. Even still, people tell me all the time how I need to say things differently in order to be heard. I have to remind them, the language they want me to use is not mine. It's the language of the *pleaser*, and it's oppressive.

So we're tired. Brown and Black people are tired. Believe me, I'm not happy with the way I get talked to, but why am I the one who has to constantly adjust? I often tell clients, "If you find me offensive, imagine what my life is like being pushed into a box since day one." Minorities are pressured to conform and punished if we don't.

In writing this book, I've been coached to speak less frankly about race, and I understand why. As the only Black person on the management team at Financial Services Inc., I had huge responsibility. I was the first and only. The criticism that bears, even from the people who looked like me, was debilitating at times. I had to play the long game because I couldn't afford to go backwards, and I refused to become a Corporate pleaser.

5. FEED THE UNSAID CURRENT

In a toxic Corporate culture, there are two existing worlds: the things people say out loud and the unsaid current. People's spoken words can be hurtful, but it's the unsaid current that leads to real trouble for brown and Black folx in Corporate. What does that mean? People will say one thing to your face and something entirely different behind your back. They'll gossip, backstab, and instigate suspicion around people's competence and worth. The GOB doesn't mind, however, because this is how they build arguments against those they aim to oppress.

For instance, HR departments are often filled with jealous people who have sometimes their first dose of power. I've seen this my whole career and experienced it firsthand. That department is supposed to be a safety zone for employees, yet their comments, insinuations, and gossip disproportionately target women and brown and Black people.

For marginalized folx, this results in paranoia. It also has a negative impact on the mental health of employees who have to deal with it. Admittedly, I've contributed to this by using the behind the scenes network. This isn't just a gossip ring, it's an actual network of recruiters and HR people who share intel on people. In hindsight, I will never do that again. I'm committed to being better and feel terrible that brown and Black people in Corporate often have no one they can speak to confidentially. Everyone reading this knows about unsaid current in their workplace. My hope is that you'll get honest about when you're participating and letting it exist.

6. MARGINALIZE THE MARGINALIZED

In my time at Financial Services Inc., Becky did everything she could to marginalize me and diminish my worth with the company. When she'd require me to do needless paperwork, when she'd enforce her ancient processes, and when she'd actively reject the progressive plans I was hired to implement, my hands would be tied. Becky's requests weren't just an annoyance, they were aimed to sabotage my success and remind me of my place as a Black woman. She wanted to keep me in an insignificant role, so she could feel more powerful.

Her staff of minions gladly joined her in dismissing my requests and adding work to my plate. Why did this happen? You see, people of color have traditionally been placed in the back office with functional roles. In other words, we're hired to clean up the crap behind white folx. The titles we are afforded have no direct correlation to profitability. Our role is to quietly ensure white people in the company look good. This is normalized exploitation.

People of color are sick of coming into these cultures where we are used, abused, and spit out without reaching management, stock options, or equal pay. To demonstrate the lack of diversity in finances companies, Harvard Business Review offers some telling statistics of Black leaders in finance. Just look at these disgraceful numbers:

2.4% are executive committee members

1.4% are managing directors

1.4% are senior portfolio managers[3]

It's even worse for women of color. The National Partnership for Women and Families reports, "Women of color in the United States experience the nation's persistent and pervasive gender wage gap most severely. The gaps represent the tangible consequences of sexism and white supremacy in the United States and how our country systematically devalues women of color and their labor."[4]

Here's how the stats currently line up for women:

- Asian American women are typically paid 87 cents for every dollar paid to white, non-Hispanic men.

- White, non-Hispanic women are typically paid just 79 cents for every dollar paid to white, non-Hispanic men.

- Black women are typically paid just 63 cents for every dollar paid to white, non-Hispanic men.

- Native American women are typically paid just 60 cents for every dollar paid to white, non-Hispanic men.

- Latinas are typically paid just 55 cents for every dollar paid to white, non-Hispanic men.[5]

The GOB cannot have equality in the workplace because they need the hierarchy to stay in power. That's why this sixth commandment is so important to recognize. Brown and Black professionals are giving their all, while white folx are earning far more, advancing their careers, and having far less stress and scrutiny. Marginalize the marginalized is a pattern you'll see in just about every workplace.

7. SMART WOMEN ARE A THREAT

White men are not threatened by the average woman or person of color in Corporate. That's because they've been raised to get whatever they want with minimal competition. But there's one group that's particularly menacing to ambitious, entitled, white men. Smart women, regardless of race, will often become the most hated person in the office.

It makes perfect sense. If the GOB's goal is to protect the white man, squelch the truth, stereotype different races, reward the pleasers, and diminish people's worth, they certainly don't want smart women to catch onto them!

I'll never forget a brilliant woman coworker named Laurie. She was smarter than any of the men leading different lines of business. She may have been the smartest person in the company. Men would openly tear her down. The insults were ruthless. In a succession meeting where Laurie was getting ripped apart, Sue once remarked, "You guys realize she was cum laude in her class, right?" They didn't care. Her intelligence made them feel mediocre, which cannot be allowed in GOB culture.

There's also a financial gate the GOB is trying to protect. The greater your education the more the company will have to pay the top of your income range. And if you keep learning and aspiring, that would mean reaching higher levels of management. This is where stocks and bonuses are often in the millions. We'll dive into compensation more in chapter five, but just realize that women and brown and Black people are cock-blocked from middle and upper management to prevent us from reaching higher levels of wealth and power. The greater our education, the more we'll demand top dollar and greater access to equity. That's not gonna fly with the GOB.

Black women in Corporate know there's a line of succession. Men are threatened by all smart women, and white women are threatened by Black women. For example, Becky sure didn't appreciate me wanting to meet Sue before accepting the job. That was a smart move on my part, and it posed a threat to Becky. It told her she wasn't good enough for me to say yes.

Once I was brought on board, Becky didn't like me pushing my business ideas, nor did she like my objections to certain tasks. Her training and certifications had been minimal. She actually got pretty far in title and income, despite her incompetence. So any woman who was more educated than she would feel the wrath of Becky's jealousy.

I decided to obtain my MBA for several reasons, but honestly, the biggest reason was to prove to myself that I was smart and capable, and that anyone questioning my intelligence would be wrong about me! It should also be said, I do not have an undergraduate degree. As a young Black girl during the 60s and 70s, I was raised to survive and get a paycheck. Education was a luxury we couldn't afford. After years of getting punched in the face because of my lack of education, I begin to absorb that into my psyche. At the same time, I also saw the mediocrity of the "educated" in Corporate. I saw the hypocrisy of the requirements they set forth for brown and Black folks that they didn't even have–education wise. Securing my MBA gave me an understanding of business and eliminated Corporate's constant demand to pay me lower wages. I wanted them to run out of excuses to marginalize me again. That's why today, I am now higher educated than most of them.

There can be a backlash to having education when you're a woman in Corporate. There was certainly a backlash to receiving my MBA–it led the jury to believe I could hop right back into Corporate and make even more money. How untrue and short sighted. Had they understood what it's like to be a woman of color, they would have given me enough money to comfortably retire.

8. DIVERSITY = WHITE WOMEN LEADERS

When you look at diversity in Corporate America, there's a clear and obvious trend–white women are prevailing under diversity initiatives. Just about every woman who has broken a glass ceiling has been white. She *also* had a boost from the men around her. This eighth commandment lets the GOB give off the illusion that they care about women, yet in reality brown and Black women are being intentionally excluded.

The elephant in the room is that white women can be sexist, they most definitely can be racist, and they are way more likely to become our bosses than us becoming theirs. This is scary stuff for people of color. Generally, white women are clueless about privilege and oppression.

Not because they want to be, because they are socially conditioned to be. We're even seeing an increase in white women supporting racism.

Look at white women who voted for Trump from 2016 to 2020. Many of these women now hold management jobs because the GOB feels safer promoting white women like that. Just because these women are not wearing a pillowcase over their faces doesn't mean they're not doing the same racist work in Corporate. And then, companies expect us to celebrate their diversity efforts which rarely ever include us!

Even today, I saw that Financial Services Inc. has hired a white woman CEO. People will applaud their efforts and cheer on this woman, but when will the GOB promote a brown or Black woman who understands how privilege and oppression works? White women aren't getting the job done. They continue to act oblivious to racial issues, while they collect their fat paychecks and add to their cashmere collections.

9. *WOMEN SHALL COMPETE*

GOB culture thrives when women compete against each other. It's why there are limited seats at the table for women. They count on us to fight over who's going to make it, instead of demanding that seats get added. Just as the other commandments serve to protect thy white man, this one makes sure women stay distracted. If our focus is taking down other women, we won't be paying attention to the

GOB's behavior and decisions. They actually want us to tear each other apart, so they can justify why women don't belong in upper management.

Remember when I mentioned being at dinner in New York City with all the guys from work, and I talked about how exhilarating it was to be surrounded by successful men? That day, I got a hint of the white woman's experience. To be surrounded by rich, powerful, white men was a glimpse into liberation. It's seductive for women. At times, we need to be accepted and liked in these circles, if only to survive. Other times, it's a ploy for power and validation.

One way to become accepted and liked is to fit the ideal description of a woman, which is what Karen did. She checked all the boxes—white, blonde, petite, smart, and pretty. White women who 'fit the description' are viewed with more innocence and backed with more force. Sure, they'll be the butt of a blonde joke here and there, but the door is open for women who fit this description. Look at television shows, such as The Bachelor. You'll see the battle to look cute. That petite blonde look is so important to women because it does pave the way. Let's be honest—white women pay serious money for hair color that can increase their bottom line. Brown and Black women don't have that luxury.

Compared to Black women's lives, white women are practically floating on clouds of ease. They get everything more easily, which they may not believe, but comparatively, it's night and day for women of color.

10. DISRUPT RACIAL PROGRESS

As we conclude these 10 Commandments, you might be thinking, "There's no way it's this bad everywhere. Racism is getting better each day!" Hmm, yes and no. Here are some alarming statistics:

Harvard Business Review says, "In fact, research shows that in the United States, the wealth gap between blacks and others continues to widen; experts predict that black families' median wealth will decrease to $0 by 2050, while that of white families will exceed $100,000."[6] This cannot be our future. Brown and Black folx refuse to be your entry level job seekers. We're done with your tokenism, exploitation, and slave/owner mentality, along with emotional abuse the GOB continually dishes out. We are done making white people more wealthy. Corporate has made baby steps in reconciling racial injustice, but on the whole, progress is still stubborn and slow.

Even those of us who do rise in Corporate America rarely do so without experiencing a simultaneous tearing down. Any signs of racial progress will be met with resistance. Someone once said to me, "The higher up the flagpole you go, the more your ass shows. The air is thin on top." It's common for people to reject new leaders, but as a Black woman, folx don't see us as leaders, so the clawing at us is even more intense. All of this hatred and fighting for power has to stop somehow.

LET'S MOVE INTO SOLUTIONS!

As you review the 10 Commandments of the GOB, realize you now have what's needed to sniff out oppression in the workplace. Now that you can see from the lens of a Black woman, you'll be a more effective ally to people of color, and you'll also feel better about yourself. None of us can feel good when we're projecting harm. We can't create misery for someone else and expect happiness to come to us.

If you don't know how GOB culture operates, you'll lack skills to fight it, you won't know who to hold accountable, and you'll continue to hurt the marginalized folx around you. Keep a list of the 10 GOB Commandments within your field of view. That will prompt you to ask yourself, "Which of these are happening in my workplace?" True healing begins when we hold each other accountable to be better and do better. We can also pledge to make these conversations about Corporate oppression the norm, not the exception.

In the next chapter, we'll discuss how to actively reject GOB culture, not just in the workplace, but in your churches, politics, schools, and communities. By now, you're likely motivated to take direct action.

"Mother, mother
There's too many of you crying
Brother, brother, brother
There's far too many of you dying
You know we've got to find a way
To bring some loving here today"

–Marvin Gaye, "What's Going On"

3

RESPONDING TO RACISM

Now that you know my story of Corporate racism and understand GOB culture, it's time to look at your own business and community. Do you know WHO's causing racial harm? Can you hear WHAT they say that's a problem? Can you see HOW their words, actions, and politics negatively impact the marginalized?

That's what we'll explore together in this chapter—how to detect your unconscious biases, fine-tune your bigot radar, understand reverse racism, and get oppressive leaders removed from politics, workplaces, nonprofits, schools, and various positions of power. Being able to identify the oppressor is crucial to the success and survival of brown and Black lives. Being able to respond appropriately is just as needed.

In the fifth chapter, we'll drill down on WHAT specific changes need to be made in Corporate to attract and keep diverse talent. But for now, let's examine some of the phrases, people, and protocols that perpetuate white supremacy in America. Until we can identify these cancers of society and unify against them, we will remain sick, divided, and unjust as a nation.

"WHY CAN'T WE HAVE A DIFFERENCE OF OPINION ANYMORE?"

There are knee-jerk phrases white people use to subtly discredit, shut down, and shame BIPOC folx who dare to discuss the racism they face. Here are the standard responses we consistently hear from people who don't understand the systemic nature of racism:

- Is it possible you're over-reacting?

- You misunderstood their intentions.

- There are only a few bad apples.

- Why must this be about race?

- Not all white people are bad.

- Just to play devil's advocate.

- Why don't you focus on the positives?

- If you said it nicely, more people would listen to you.

- Isn't what you're saying reverse racism?

Notice how these phrases aim to define what's racist and what's not. They take evidence, history, and research pointing to decades of white supremacy and claim it's been fabricated, exaggerated, and used against them. They act as if my message is radical, unique to me. They call my experience at Financial Services Inc. an "unfortunate occurrence" and declare that people are inherently good. Then, they'll try to teach me how to focus on positivity, or they'll recommend a book about how to get my message across more effectively. If I keep talking about race, that's when they'll accuse me of getting upset, or they'll act like I've personally attacked them. To end their misery, they'll say, "Let's just agree to disagree," or "Why can't people have a difference of opinion anymore?"

I have to explain that not everyone's opinion is worthy. Opinions don't require facts, nor do they require experience in another person's shoes. Plus, some people's opinions perpetuate violence and oppression. We're now able to categorize a person's opinions as racist, sexist, homophobic, elitist, xenophobic, ageist, fatphobic, ableist, etc., according to mountains of data and real life stories that reflect how damaging those opinions actually are.

We don't need to grow tolerance for people's opinions. We need to get on the same page about what is unacceptable and start holding people accountable. This isn't about silencing or punishing anyone, it's about creating a society where power is shared, brown and Black people are safe, and everyone can thrive. This thing is, you can't wait around for everyone to jump on board. It starts with you, right this second.

WHAT DO YOU THINK WHEN YOU FIRST MEET ME?

When we meet someone, we have a notion about who they might be and how they might act, talk, dress, or live based on their gender, sexuality, race, class, occupation, or religion. It's human nature to look for similarities when interacting with different types of people, yet if we only see stereotypes, we shield ourselves from the truth about who this person actually is. We also assign characteristics onto that person that are probably untrue and harmful to perpetuate. In other words, our hidden thoughts are likely oppressive to someone. And although they might exist without our full awareness, they still come through in our body language, tone of voice, and snap assessments of people and situations.

Unconscious bias training helps you see the messages that reside in your psyche—those you've received from society and those you've created throughout life. Most people would deny being hateful. Just as most people wouldn't brag about being racist, but their unabashed loyalty to white supremacist policies says otherwise. White America has been programmed to view Black people in a negative light. It takes intentional work to notice the narrative you might have assigned onto any person of color, along with a message you've been taught to believe.

It's not always societal programming that shapes our thoughts. Our firsthand experiences do as well. My history with white women has my guard up 24/7, but if I believed all white women sought to destroy me, it would block the chance for friendships, business, and allies. With that said, my gut-wrenching reaction to white women is still there because their harm is the norm, not the exception, for me and the majority of Black women.

When we don't slow down and ask what's happening in our heads, we can naturally jump to conclusions and try to put others in a box, whether we mean to or not. We all have unconscious biases. The goal is to make them *conscious* and choose a thought that's more kind and true before opening your mouth or taking action.

It can be hard to accept what you discover in your unconscious. White people freak out when accused of having racist thoughts, yet their racial biases are a given. We live in a racist society. It's all around us! When you own that, it frees you from the shame of being called a racist. Instead of rejecting this label, realize it's the truth of the America to which you belong. Even the most progressive cities have blatant acts of racism that go unchecked. There's so much work yet to be done, and it starts when you can uncover the harmful thoughts in your head, ponder their oppressive origins, and collectively agree on what's unacceptable.

My father was born and raised during the Jim Crow era in the South. He and his family picked cotton in the fields day and night. His childhood tales of sweat and hard work are sealed into my brain. He went on to join the Air Force, get a paralegal degree, and become a union leader. I used to type his homework for him in the middle of the night and listen to his stories of the racists in charge of everything. What my father endured and ultimately died from in 2003 was a lifetime of fight. The disease that killed him was a manifestation of the stressors of being a Black man—all those years of having to swallow his pride and exist in a culture that doesn't place importance on his life.

Every day, still, Black men get murdered, taunted, stalked, and imprisoned by the police, while white people sit around criticizing and questioning why they fled from the cops in the first place. What would you do if a gun was pointed to your head, and you could be killed without having done anything wrong, just like thousands before you? When your adrenaline is soaring and the moment feels like life or death, wouldn't you instinctively run?

Most white people nod in agreement, never having considered the Black person's experience, nor the toll it's taken on our mental, emotional, and physical health. They expect Black people to be model citizens in the face of death, yet even when we *are* model citizens, we still get taken down. When you accuse Black women of being angry, you're damn right we're angry. You would be too if you were worried sick about your family getting unfairly accused, arrested, and killed.

Do you think Black people are less capable?

Do you bet that we'll fail before we succeed?

Do you expect us to be in secondary positions, rather than leadership?

Do you think Black folx can't be trusted?

Do you fear we're going to get loud, angry, or mean?

Do you view Black folx as uneducated and misguided?

Do you think Black people in charge will go on a power trip?

Do you fear Black people will do to white people what they've done to us?

White people are offended when they're perceived as the oppressor, although Black people didn't make up those stereotypes about ourselves. They were created to keep us unstable and submissive. After all, if we believe we are broken, then we will gratefully take the crumbs white people in power are offering. Enforcing stereotypes is how power gets asserted and maintained. To fight back, you have to stop judging the ones being harmed and oppressed. Instead, look at the system and the people who are oppressing us. Stop asking brown and Black people not to get upset by racism. Instead, take a hard look at the damage being done to us with all this denial and deflection.

When Black people get labeled a "performance problem" in Corporate, does anyone really understand what's going on with them?

When Black people get accused of being "unprofessional," do we question whose standards of professionalism are being placed on them?

When Black people are deemed "aggressive" or "unapproachable," is there anyone in the room to say that's a racist assessment?

Even "good" white leaders have implicit views about people of color. Anyone who thinks this isn't happening in their organization is naive. As you search your psyche for implicit bias, it's also important to hear projection. Projection is a common term in the psychology field. It basically means, what we find abhorrent in others are often traits we refuse to acknowledge in ourselves. There's a quote I used in my TEDx Talk that summarizes projection: *I am not who you think I am. You are who you think I am.*[1]

So when a leader gets feedback about a brown or Black person, they must stop and realize what the sender of that message has just revealed. They've given you access to their insecurities, shortcomings, and the feelings they harbor towards others. For instance, when Karen and Becky got on the witness stand against me, they believed everything they said. They saw me as angry, vindictive, conniving, and untrustworthy, and that's also a projection of what they're unwilling to see in themselves.

Throughout my years in Human Resources, I heard projections every day from people aiming to get what they want. They would take a variety of stereotypes and use them to invalidate their coworkers. And while they thought they were doing me a favor by acting as the "unsaid current," they were merely showing me what they couldn't see in themselves.

So once again, not all opinions are created equal, and your unconscious thoughts must not go unchecked. This is how you make your assessments of people increasingly more true and effective. It's how you cease to marginalize and hurt brown and Black individuals. This next suggestion might make you cringe, but I implore you to get ready to take decisive action with the most harmful people in your sphere.

YOU NEED TO REMOVE THE BIGOTS.

If people of color are important to your diversity efforts, it's not going to happen while bigots are in leadership. Oh, they are there. Believe me! Bigots, in my definition, aren't just racist, they're sexist, ableist, ageist, homophobic, transphobic. They've bought into all of it. Some bigots are more flagrant than others. You have to know who they are and be able to identify them as such. Remember, we have to get on the same page about what and who is unacceptable.

You might not know offhand who poses a threat in your company or community. That's because bigots are skilled at carrying themselves in publicly acceptable ways, as they gossip, manipulate, and scheme to ensure their own success. Bigots are frequently your "high-producing" people. They are masters at managing up and often have strong P&L statements. Their contributions to the company's bottom line allow their damaging behaviors to be ignored. After all, no one wants to touch someone who is raking in dough for the business. However, there is a cost in people and profitability when they are kept on board.

Companies can no longer say, "We can't just fire these people! What if they sue us?" You have to realize–the company is already taking a risk with brown and Black people who've had to put up with racism at work all this time. Inaction will become a no-win situation for everyone, except the bigot. You cannot let them remain. Bigots don't do it just because they "hate," they do it to keep their dominance intact. They don't want to evolve, so don't fool yourself into believing they do, or that you have to give them a chance to change. That will only prolong the suffering they cause. It's the American way to say no to Black people. Start saying no to bigots in every industry and facet of community, and just watch how the energy is uplifted.

We cannot abolish bigots completely, I'm sorry to say. They will always exist, but we do need to perform a demotion of sorts. It starts with recognizing who they are in your organization. Start looking at the top. When you give a person with unchecked biases some clout, the pattern of oppression can easily kick into gear. This person will become more empowered to keep going. One bigoted leader or employee can impact the culture for years to come. Companies need to see them as immediate liabilities. The safety of people must be front and center—now!

If you can't clearly identify the bigots in your organization, reach out to people of color who have freely left or have been fired. Listen to what they say, and also ask brown and Black people who are still in the company. Let them confidentially offer feedback. Every marginalized group has raised issues through HR over the years, and in many cases, but particularly for brown and Black folx, *they* were painted as troublemakers, drama queens, negative thinkers, and performance problems. Make sure this doesn't happen again!

Knowing the oppressive ways of GOB, doesn't it make sense to incentivize anyone for coming forward with information on bigots? This person could save you millions by naming a source of danger and disgruntlement in the office.

Whistleblowers have had a tough road through history, but they are instrumental to truth being disseminated.

By the way, if you don't know what to say in these conversations, here are some responses that could be helpful. Depending on your relationship with that person, this could be all you need to say while collecting information about people's instances with racism and oppression:

1. I fully hear you.

2. Thanks for what you've shared.

3. How do you recommend we address this?

4. How can we properly right these wrongs?

5. What other observations do you have about the company?

6. What obstacles can I remove for you?

7. How can I amplify you?

8. Is there anything I need to stop doing?

9. How would you like to be compensated for this conversation?

Can you feel the difference between these and the earlier responses? Notice the gratitude, openness, specificity, and honoring nature of these replies. Print this list and post it on the wall in your office. When you have these conversations, take copious notes and pay an anti-racism expert to answer your questions. It's okay to need help with what you don't understand. You may also need help digesting what you've been told. All of that is fine. What isn't okay is ignoring it, failing to seek guidance, and not taking action. Get used to asking, listening, believing, and changing, rather than demanding, defending, protecting, and dismissing.

Remember the goal isn't to punish white people, it's to have a safe and productive space for brown and Black professionals at work—a place where everyone is on the same page about what is unacceptable. Let the bigots learn a valuable lesson through accountability and firing. Let people of color breathe a sigh of relief knowing another bigot has left the building. It's the least you can do.

THERE'S NO SUCH THING AS REVERSE RACISM.

Before we continue, I know what you might be thinking. "Isn't it reverse racism to target white people?" Thank you for asking. This is such an important distinction to learn. Worku Nida, an expert in sociocultural anthropology, says we must first break down the roots of racism in the U.S. "Racism is a mechanism where resources and unfortunately power, wealth, prestige, and even humanity are distributed along a color line."[2]

"My practice and knowledge is that racism is the combination of two things: discrimination plus power over," said Lynne Lyman, a justice advocate and director of Drug Policy

Alliance. She continued, "Where a lot of white people get caught up and confused is that they may have felt discriminated against... but it's very different from racism when you don't have the power. Racism can only come from the most dominant group."[3]

You wouldn't believe how many people can't have a conversation about racism without blabbing, "Not all white people," or "Aren't you being racist towards white people?" No, there's no such thing as reverse racism. Racism requires one side having power over another. People of color don't have that power. Most often, low-income, limited-education white people seem to feel the most discrimination. They'll talk about getting teased as kids, blocked from college scholarships, and passed over for promotions as adults. That's not reverse racism. That's about getting bullied and not getting what you think you deserve as a white person.

With that said, let's keep going in our quest to eradicate oppression in Corporate and communities. Now that you know the phrases, people, and protocols that perpetuate white supremacy in America, and you understand how white women can strengthen the plight of the patriarchy, we need to get even more specific about the bigotry they promote.

"A nation planted, so concerned with gain
As the seasons come and go, greater grows the pain
And far too many feelin the strain
When will there be a harvest for the world"

–Isley Brothers, "Harvest for the World"

WHITE WOMEN

So far, you've heard my personal story of racism in Corporate America, you've learned how Good Ole Boys culture keeps oppression alive, you examined your thoughts and responses to racism, and you have prepared to remove the bigots who reside in leadership. It's time to face the most heated topic in this book—white women's harm.

This chapter is going to be raw and real, and please know, I'm trying to be respectful. This is the hardest issue to discuss because no matter how kind and clear I try to be, white people will inevitably make me the villain in this conversation. And yet, I'm willing to take the punches because my people of color have suffered tremendously due to white women's harm. We desperately need to talk about how it looks, sounds, and feels, so we can get on the same page about what's unacceptable and do something about it!

Before we begin, I want you to know—there are *many* white women who support me. Not only do they stand with me, they welcome this conversation because their experiences with white women have been problematic too. White women allies want to know what their sisters of color need from them. They want to heal the divide and take responsibility for their part. Men thank me for this conversation as well. They see power struggles between women, but they don't know when or how to get involved, particularly in the workplace. This chapter will offer direction, regardless of your gender.

White women play a major role in upholding systems of oppression. They have extraordinary power. When they use their privilege to protect and promote the marginalized, the rewards can be transformative for absolutely everyone, including them. That's why we must spend extra time on this touchy subject.

White women have a choice in how they use their power. The goal of this chapter is to show them how to use it wisely. It's also to show you, the reader, how to determine which women deserve leadership positions, and which of them do not. White people have to gain this sense of discernment immediately. I hope my examples in this chapter reveal the urgency to stop white women's racial harm.

THE CRISIS IN WOMEN'S LEADERSHIP

In 2013, Sheryl Sandberg, Chief Operating Officer of Facebook, released her bestselling book, *Lean In: Women, Work, and the Will to Lead*. Like the majority of white women authors before her, Sandberg wrote a guide for wealthy, married, heterosexual, white women in Corporate—and yet, it was packaged as a guide for ALL professional women.[1]

It seems Sandberg didn't consider if her advice was applicable to women of color. It appears she might not even have asked us, nor was she pressured to do so. It didn't matter though. Without representation of Black and brown women's history, health, family life, and reality in America, Sandberg's book was hailed as a Godsend to professional women. It rode the New York Times best seller's list for more than a year and landed Sandberg on the covers of *Time* and *Fortune*, not to mention solid media exposure and lucrative speaking gigs. The *Lean In* splash was more like a tsunami. People still praise it today.

Journalist Connie Schultz offered some initial critiques in the *Washington Post*. "*Lean In* reads like a book that was written too soon. Sandberg is thinking out loud, bouncing from idea to idea, full of good intentions but bubbling with contradictions: Stand up for yourself, but don't tick off the boss. Seek help from more experienced women, but don't ask for a mentor. Make your husband a real partner, but don't tell him how to do it." Schultz said Sandberg also believed that women generally fall behind in their careers because of their own bad choices.[2]

You might be thinking, "Okay, fine. She wrote a book that was laced with privilege and wasn't progressive enough. At least we're talking about it now in 2021. Right?" It's not that simple.

- Do you think a Black woman would have gotten away with writing a mediocre book that claimed to apply to all women? Nope.

- Do you think we would have been sought out by a book publisher, paid a healthy advance, and given an outpouring of visibility and high-paying speaking opportunities? Nope.

- Would a Black woman have been offered a Corporate position like Sandberg's, and would she have been crowned with automatic credibility as leader for ALL women? Nope.

As an author and business leader, Sandberg made the critical error of assuming all women were basically the same, which can no longer be acceptable. Not only did she erase color, she barely considered the needs of the LGBTQ community. She also failed to properly acknowledge single parents, trauma survivors, neurodivergent folx, or differently abled and childfree women. Her book wasn't about empowerment, it was about propelling white women into leadership and enforcing dominant culture norms.

Even though this book was an insult to Black women and other marginalized groups, *Lean In* "Circles" sprung up around the country–led by white professional women hailing themselves as leaders. Black women had no time or interest in these white feminist groups. We were too busy working two jobs, caring for our families, and earning 63 cents on the dollar to the white man.[3] There's no doubt white women were advancing through Sandberg's suggestions, and that's not to say they were "sticking it to the man" either. As you've now learned, Good Ole Boys culture will promote a white woman knowing she's more likely to play their oppressive games.

It doesn't stop there. *Lean In* propelled a boom of white women Corporate speakers, life coaches, and trainers slinging all kinds of white women's bullshit. Companies paid top dollar to infuse Sandberg-style philosophies into the workplace. All along, Black women had to play along with a smile. If we tried to explain why this did not apply to the Black woman's experience, our words would be deemed negative and critical. White women would argue we were all affected by sexism, therefore, women need to stick together.

That's what Black women have been telling them all along, but because we were asking *them* to change, they think we're being mean and divisive.

White women will talk freely about the poor treatment they receive from men, yet when called out on their behavior towards Black and brown women, they think it's their right to decide what's racist or not. They do not own up to what they cannot see about themselves. And when they do, they'll tell you through tears it was never their intention, and their words were misconstrued.

White women also play naive when confronted with stats about their advancement before ours. I saw a recent article from *Fortune* titled, "The number of female CEOs in the Fortune 500 hits an all-time record." I hoped for good news for women of color, but my fears were confirmed:

> "Within the ranks of the 37 women who make up this list, a longstanding problem persists: there is starkly little racial diversity. Only three of the 37 are women of color." Even worse, "Not one of the 500 companies on the list has a black woman at the helm."[4]

Since then, Roz Brewer, a Black woman leader from Starbucks, became CEO of Walgreens.[5] That's a step in the right direction, but our progress needs to be expedited. Without representation and access to wealth, Black financial futures will continue to be both limited and uncertain.

Even so, white women expect us to ignore the facts and keep helping them succeed. Those days are done!

- With seemingly no easy way to talk about white women's harm, how are we going to repair this divide?

- If we can't talk about what's broken and how it happened, how will we know what to build next?

- How can white women's harm possibly get better when *only* people of color can see what's going on?

These questions illuminate why there's a whole chapter on this topic. I'm counting on white women to step up and see the big picture here. I'm also hoping my sisters of color are feeling validated right now. Many of you have been dying to say this stuff forever, but couldn't out of fear of punishment.

WHITE WOMEN'S RACISM ISN'T NEW.

When you think of slave owners, do you envision white men? Most white people do, but you need to consider the white woman's role. They have a long history of diminishing Black individuals. They owned slaves too, and while Black women fed their babies, cooked their food, and cleaned their homes, white women treated us like dogs. White women grabbed for wealth and power, just like men. Difference was, the women were painted as pure, innocent, and in need of protection. This view of white women still persists today. The root of the problem may be that white girls are raised with a princess mentality, while Black and brown women are raised to be warriors–fierce, resilient, and discerning. The difference in our upbringing is important to note.

All women deserve to be free of violence and abuse, but white women learned that in the name of their protection, they could gain power too. Emmett Till was a 14-year-old Black boy from Mississippi. In 1955, a white woman falsely accused Emmett of grabbing her in a sexually crude manner. Emmett was punished by two white men who dragged his body behind a moving truck, thus ending his life. Those two killers were let off the hook by an all-male, all-white jury.

How do I know she lied? She admitted it about 50 years later.[6] She had positioned herself as meek and afraid, but that wasn't true. She had power that was freely and un-apologetically used to have a beautiful, innocent, Black boy pulverized beyond recognition. She was the catalyst to his tragic demise, just like millions of Karens in Corporate and communities.

In 2020, a young white woman was walking her dog in Central Park. A Black gentleman calmly asked her to leash up her dog. While dialing 911, Amy Cooper said, "I'm going to tell them an African American man is threatening my life!" As the operator answered, Cooper's voice went from "don't fuck with me, Black man," to exasperated damsel in distress.[7]

At that moment, Ms. Cooper believed the dog leash rules didn't apply to her, and she didn't like having to take orders from a Black man either, so she made herself the victim. When the video of Cooper went viral, that's when she finally realized how badly she screwed up. She told the news, her "entire life is being destroyed right now."[8] Obviously, Amy Cooper still has some things to learn about *her* power to destroy as a white woman.

Black women are terrified for our boys. We live in fear of the police, but we're also terrified of what these conniving and calculating white women can do to our men. How pathetic is that? We have to teach our sons about what can and will be done to them.

When my son Aaron was in middle school, a (white) girl made an accusation against him. When he was called to the principal's office, Aaron was devastated. He explained his words and actions had been taken out of context. I knew then it was time to have the "white girl talk" with him. Like every Black mom in America, I had to tell my teenage son about Emmett Till and the danger of white girls. "They'll get you in trouble and crush everything you've worked so hard to achieve."

Before Aaron left for Stanford on a basketball scholarship, I had to remind him again that he's a star, and white girls will stop at nothing to associate with someone of his caliber. I told him, "They will take you down, if you reject or offend them. They will compete to be with you, and they will hold you accountable if outcomes don't land in their favor." I used to keep Aaron from parties in high school at the rich, Bellevue, white girls' houses. He would get so mad at me, but today, he's fully aware of why I needed to protect him, and why he needed to protect himself.

EVEN THE "WOKE" ONES CAN BE PROBLEMATIC.

An infuriating example of white women's harm is Robin DiAngelo, author of *White Fragility: Why It's So Hard for White People to Talk About Racism*. Like Sheryl Sandberg, DiAngelo has also become a New York Times bestseller. Her book about racism is no different than what Black anti-racism educators have said for years. But since DiAngelo is white, white people will listen to her. Corporate America clamored to hire her at $22,000 for a 3.5-hour speech.[9] I'm not criticizing her for making money, but she's doing it at the expense of Black antiracist educators.

Black women in my field have to fight to get $10,000 speaker fees, when white women like DiAngelo get paid more than twice that amount. I'm not asking her to cease her antiracism business. I'm asking her to be an example of what she teaches. She should have negotiated additional fees to bring her Black colleagues along. DiAngelo could have introduced Corporate America to an incredible network of

Black professionals, artists, educators, and activists. Instead, she took the money and credit for herself.

My friend Alice teaches Boot Camp for women who want to develop their voices in leadership. As a white woman with a vast support system, she makes a point to help me get speaking opportunities. Alice recently asked if I wanted to speak at a group of (mostly) white and wealthy business women. She sent an introduction email to the head of the group, and they came back saying, "We don't think Cindi is qualified." Alice replied, "Oh, I must have sent the wrong website." She resent my link. "No, you gave us the right one," they said. "We saw this already."

Alice was dumbfounded. She tried to explain that in many ways, I'm more qualified than she. They said, "We're going to need Cindi to lay out her talk for us." They wanted to review the language I was using to convey my message about racism. When this request showed up in my inbox, I promptly hit reply all: "I will not be disclosing my agenda." That was the end of that.

Now, you see, Alice doesn't speak on race, but she can pull in $5,000-10,000 per talk because a.) her training doesn't threaten those in power, and b.) experience and education do not matter as much when you're white. I have an executive MBA, three decades in Corporate HR, a long-standing radio show, *and* I ran for public office and am known for being an active voice for race. Yet those hoity toity, white women *still* considered Alice more qualified than me. You might be like, "What? That can't be." See, you think this is an anomaly, but it's the norm. Black women have to prove ourselves repeatedly, while less qualified, white women slide into positions and get paid handsomely.

My experience with this white women's group is merely a glimpse into what it's like as a Black woman entrepreneur, executive, or nonprofit employee. Our path to success takes three to five times as long as white women, through no fault of our own. Alice got to see firsthand how white women scrutinize, discriminate, and act as gatekeepers. She also saw the urgency that's needed to advocate for women of color and disrupt these double standards.

Did you know nonprofit leadership is 90% white?[10] Just like in Human Resources, those numbers are undoubtedly skewed towards women. This percentage reveals an important distinction–white women are rarely interested in social justice, unless it promotes them and makes them look like a savior. That might sound harsh, but let it sink in, if you must.

I asked a white woman nonprofit CEO if she would have taken that position without the Executive Director title–she couldn't answer. That's because her answer was likely no. If she can't wear the crown, her empathy for the marginalized will start to dwindle. I've had other white women friends privately admit the same. If they were going to volunteer, they wanted to lead in some capacity.

White women work in nonprofits because they want to do something meaningful, and many of them want to *look* like they're doing something good and pious. In reality, what's meaningful to them is the title. If they cared for the cause, they would insist on having people of color lead these groups. We know the issues of impoverished communities firsthand and can much better relate to ones who are struggling.

You might think white people (or white women) get these jobs because they can generate funding. That is true. Black-led nonprofits are underfunded compared to white-led. The Bridgespan Group did a study showing "revenues of the Black-led organizations are 24 percent smaller than the revenues of their white-led counterparts, and the unrestricted net assets of the Black-led organizations are 76 percent smaller than their white-led counterparts."[11]

So if white women nonprofit leaders are so successful at getting money, why are nonprofits always struggling? Why don't their results show? Is this about fixing the systemic racism Black and brown communities face, or is it about propelling another white woman into a position of power that she cannot (or will not) fix?

WHITE WOMEN CAN LITERALLY CHANGE AMERICA.

When we propel women into office or leadership positions, we have to discern which are worthy. Look at Supreme Court Justice Amy Comey Barrett. She isn't accomplished enough to hold such a prestigious title, though her privilege makes her believe she is. She partnered with a racist pig of a president to further an agenda that could destroy the lives of the marginalized for decades.

Her validation of an abusive leader and brazen sense of entitlement is no different than white women all over the country who vote oppressive white men into office. Instead of standing in unity with all women, they stand behind the wealthy to diminish women's rights and to strip away protections and advancements of non-dominant culture groups. Why does liberation of the marginalized upset them? Because they benefit from their oppression. That's what's going on there. We have to stop being baffled by these women. I'm telling you what's up with them!

If you look at Black women, we are united in how we vote and what we deem as vital to protect. Less than 6% of Black women voted for Trump in 2016, and less than 10% in 2020.[12] Do you notice the upward trend in voting for racism? That's why this chapter exists. White women's harm appears to be worsening. Black women know there's power in our votes too. That's why there is such a massive attempt to suppress voters. If they can shut us up, they can take away our power.

Our democracy is under attack by white people upholding voter suppression and stripping voters' rights. Black women politicians like Stacey Abrams weren't going to let that happen in her state of Georgia. In fact, Black votes are what ultimately elected Joe Biden.

If white women would join forces with Black women, heck, even if you would unite as white women together, just imagine the utopia that we could create for our kids, communities, and collective safety. In areas of education, affordable housing, income, religion, and taxes, we could focus on what matters most:

- Public education would no longer fail Black and brown kids. ALL children would get the chance to learn and be fed.

- Public funds would flow to charter schools that welcome Black kids, providing further alternatives in the education system.

- Candidates and elected officials could talk frankly about the necessary changes without financial punishments from unions and Corporate donors.

- Pastors and churches would call out white supremacy directly and hold its members accountable for their racism, despite the tithings they offer.

- While pay gaps equalize and minimum wage rises, lower-income people would pay a smaller share of their income in taxes than the wealthy.

- Renters and low income families would have affordable housing available that was truly affordable and not hard to find.

Systems against brown and Black people are beginning to crumble and take new shape, but help is still greatly needed. We need white women to demonstrate their understanding of systemic racism in order to be considered for leadership of any kind. She must also demonstrate that she's done some personal work around her own ingrained racism and sexism. After all, change starts from within, and we're all affected by oppression in this country.

START WITH YOURSELF.

There's a point in every feminist's life when she discovers how she's being controlled by the patriarchy, and how she's keeping her own oppression alive. When white women have this information, they can literally move mountains with their anger and determination. I'm hoping this chapter has a similar effect because woke, white women can truly become our friends.

The white women I know who are safe, aware, and helpful have spent time researching the history of racism, they've examined how it exists in their industries, neighborhoods, and families, and they're committed to becoming allies to people of color. White women say they want to get on board with us, but they don't know how. Hopefully these examples will show you the way.

White women are the number one demographic for personal growth, so antiracism work shouldn't be new territory for them. It's really a matter of wanting to evolve and getting humble about what they were not taught, or what they've chosen to reject. A white person can study racism until the end of time, but those who make progress do one distinguishable thing—they get truthful about how they feel about themselves first.

White women, are you truly happy with your lives? Do you know who you are? Do you have self-agency? Do you love yourself unconditionally? The majority of professional white women I know seem hyper-focused on their looks. When they greet each other, they instantly evaluate each other's hair, make-up, shoes, purse, outfit, and weight. White women are always sizing each other up, as they are pushed to make themselves more pleasing to the male gaze. They aim to "fit the description," so they can feel liked, accepted, and safe.

The media keeps the beauty standard in place as well. White, blonde women get the majority of ad space, jobs, and attention. Why do you think so many white women bleach their hair? To belong. To get hired. To be viewed as "pretty," according to white American standards.

We're finally seeing a change in who gets represented on the screen, which is an opportunity for white women to revolt and refuse the Barbie doll standard. They could advocate for brown and Black voices and bodies to be showcased, heard, seen, and paid well. They could step aside and reclaim who they truly are, and what they truly want to look like without societal pressure.

GOOD WHITE WOMEN DO EXIST.

Yes, magnificent white women absolutely exist. My attorney in the trial was an excellent example. When she looked at me in court and said, "I'm your warrior now," it was a pivotal moment in my healing. I was so used to fighting for myself. To watch this smart and skilled woman take the floor, work the room, and catch people in their lies was the hug I needed most. She basically said, "Let me take care of this for you." Yes, I was paying her, but the manner in which she stepped up to the plate gave me a vision of what's possible for other white women.

My friend Amelia is a stellar example of an advocate for Black and brown women. As chairwoman of a nonprofit board, Amelia temporarily took the helm when the CEO retired. She did this to ensure a person of color got into the seat next. Aside from the tangible acts of activism she performs, she also knows how to be a friend to a Black woman. What I appreciate about Amelia:

She is not offended by real talk with me. She asks the right questions. She's not defensive about white women's harm. She seeks my counsel. She accepts what I say as truth. She doesn't try to justify her points of view. She listens, not just one time, but repeatedly. She's willing to make business introductions for me. She checks on me when I'm sick or down. I don't have to teach her to care, she automatically does.

Amelia started a phenomenal women's group to which I belong. This crew is mostly white women. Through this year of COVID lockdowns, I've been touched by the ways we've showed up for each other and reached out for support. If women came together in these circles of trust and safety, our country would completely transform for the better. I'm certain of it.

My friend Julie works for one of the major tech companies in the Pacific Northwest. She prompted them to invest money with me as a radio sponsor and client. Julie is also connected to someone who controls the author network for their company. She told them, "We have to go to bat for Cindi," and positioned me as an essential speaker for employee and management training. That's what being an ally looks like, right there.

Hillary Clinton is a white woman hero to me. Many can't stand her, but I respect her and what she's endured. Hillary knows what it means to be a woman who spearheads change. She knows how it feels to have the wolves come after you for every little thing you do. Hillary just kept lifting her head high, and I think more white women would do good by watching Hillary's style.

The more racial justice work I do, the more evolved, white women I find. However, even in activism groups, white women will inevitably use their whiteness as a weapon. To conclude this chapter, here are few action steps for white women to show their understanding of systemic oppression, and to get on board with their sisters of color. This list should also be helpful to men who want to spot white women's harm and end it in their organizations and communities.

15 CRUCIAL STEPS TO END WHITE WOMEN'S HARM:

1. Stop. Just stop this atrocious behavior, and realize you are harming not just people of color, but also yourself, your daughters, and their children's children by passing on this abusive pattern of racism.

2. Listen. Historically and habitually, white women have refused to sit back, shut up, and listen when called into racial conversations. They make

everything about them and are quick to justify their opinions and behaviors.

3. Review. Look at your history with Black, indigenous, and people of color. How did your family view race? What did your parents, teachers, coaches, and community leaders teach you about Black people?

4. Inquire. When you read about "Karens" and white women's harm, don't brush it off with a laugh or critique. Ask yourself, "Have I ever done that? Who do I know who has? What should I have done instead?"

5. Challenge. Call out the racism, sexism, and all forms of oppression around you–friends, family, coworkers, and even the Board of Directors. Your voice is needed and long overdue.

6. Submit. Projecting an air of superiority is a tool of white supremacy. Notice when you think you're right about race, or when you look to white people only for answers to your racial questions.

7. Sacrifice. Learn to step aside and give your resources to people of color. Risk losing something.

8. Learn. Watch how Black women celebrate each other and have a united force. Take note of how we support ourselves, each other, and our communities at large.

9. Discern. Hire white leaders based on their understanding of white women's harm and all forms of oppression. Don't give *anyone* power who hasn't taken measurable steps to support people of color

and abolish racism.

10. Normalize. Don't make this conversation taboo. Sit down with white women and examine the harm you see in your work, lives, and heart. Make it part of the discussion in women's groups and families.

11. Promote. Get Black women into senior leadership roles, and make sure we are paid the same as every white man—including bonuses and stock options (more on that in the next chapter). Also, make sure we are protected in those positions.

12. Reject. Stop supporting all-white women's conferences that don't feature women of color. Stop buying books from white women who don't actively support women of color. Unsubscribe from their newsletters.

13. Demand. Advocate for diversity on the billboards and screens, and stop handing opportunities to women who fit patriarchal standards.

14. Help. Make it your mission to get Black women paid. When you know of an opportunity that traditionally goes to white women, pause, then offer that opportunity to a Black woman and make sure it's hers.

15. Prosecute. Here's a solution for the cop-calling Karens of America. Put a system in place to identify and punish these women (or anyone) for sabotaging brown and Black lives, including in Corporate America!

I hope white women will receive my words as an invite to join a revolution. When you help Black and brown women rise, we all rise. You also break a pattern of abuse that's being passed down to your children and is damaging our children of color. White women are stepping up to the plate as fierce advocates. Find these groups and start doing what it takes to elevate the collective "us." And while you're at it, please don't ever forget what you've learned about white women's harm throughout history, and how it's still being repeated today. You're not being asked to live in the past, but rather to see how much hasn't changed.

In the next chapter, we'll shift back to Corporate to reveal the essential areas of transformation needed. Protecting and promoting people of color in the workplace is not only vital for our safety and success, there's increasing pressure to make it happen. While my suggestions so far have been somewhat loose, we're going to get specific about what you need to know to crush racism in Corporate America.

"They say this mountain can't be moved
They say these chains will never break
But they don't know You like we do
There is power in Your name"

–Ceci Winans, "Believe"

OPEN THE GATES OF WEALTH AND POWER

Let me define Corporate America for you: Corporate America is a capitalistic system where shareholder profit is of primary concern and obtained through destructive measures that prevent brown and Black people from reaching the same levels of wealth and power as their white counterparts.

Corporate has an opportunity to end this trajectory, and it's not so much an option anymore because diversity, equity, and inclusion have proven to make logical, financial, and statistical sense. When you lift up the most marginalized, everyone else rises. Black leaders, in particular, have been explaining this possibility for decades. Thankfully, in 2021, tolerance for racism is on the decline, and the pressure is mounting on corporations to get antiracism training, at minimum. These inescapable changes, whether forced or not, still require courage.

This chapter will help you become aware of the specific areas of racism and oppression in Corporate. By pointing our fingers in the right places, we can make quick, impactful shifts that enable our cultures and communities to work for everyone.

My ideas in this section might seem extreme or impossible to you. That's because you've probably never imagined how companies would need to function without white supremacy. My ideas might also seem anti-business to you. That's because you've likely never looked at business from an equity lens.

I love business, I'm good at business, I own a business, and I'm a champion for business. My goal isn't to inflict punishment on business. It's to help companies evolve into pro-people AND pro-profit entities. Both are possible!

Before we continue, let's review what you've encountered in this book so far. You've heard my personal story about Corporate racism, you've learned about Good Ole Boys culture and white women's harm, and you've grown in detecting how racism gets deflected and denied. Now that you've been given plenty of context and history, my suggestions for crushing Corporate racism will probably make sense to you. Take these ideas to your focus groups, action committees, and leadership circles. They are starting points and visions for what ultimately needs to happen in Corporate.

RACISM IS NOW COSTLY

We have finally come to the point where there's a literal price to pay for minimizing the potential of people of color at work. Corporate policies, practices, and protocols need to be rewritten immediately. Companies who bypass the seriousness of what's at stake will not be happy with their future results, and their leaders' days will be numbered. McKinsey and Company share copious research on the success of diversity initiatives. Here you see both sides of the coin:

> "Overall, companies in the bottom quartile for both gender and ethnic/cultural diversity were 29% less likely to achieve above-average profitability." Conversely, "Companies in the top quartile for ethnic/cultural diversity on executive teams were 33% more likely to have industry-leading profitability."[1]

No longer is there a viable excuse to reject education around how to include brown and Black professionals. Organizations must board the antiracism train immediately. Any business that's just starting now has already lost quality people of color and done significant harm to our health and wealth.

Black leaders have been forced to keep their chins up. Now, we are now exiting institutions that refuse to evolve–like philosopher Cornel West who recently said goodbye to

Harvard after being passed over for tenure.[2] Years ago, it would seem unthinkable to snub one of the world's most acclaimed schools. Today, it's not unusual.

In the Seattle area, Dr. Ben Danielson, a celebrated Black doctor, walked away, accusing his former employer, Seattle Children's, of racism. Danielson made the statement, "The institution is replete with racism and a disregard for people who don't look like them in leadership."[3] Notice he didn't mince words. Black leaders are tired of being polite. Corporations don't get to play with our lives any more.

THE LIE OF LIMITED POOLS

Wells Fargo's CEO, Charles Scharf, recently made an irrational comment about the company's diversity efforts. He said, "While it might sound like an excuse, the unfortunate reality is that there is a very limited pool of black talent to recruit from with this specific experience as our industry does not have enough diversity in most senior roles."[4] "A very limited pool" he says? Don't believe this man's age-old excuse. Black and brown candidates are rarely advantaged in the hiring process. The reasons for this inequity are plentiful:

- White decision makers often have white-only networks.

- They usually assume inferiority in people of color.

- They expect diverse people to recruit their own kind.

- They aren't required to have cultural competency.

- They aren't trusted by people of color.

Did you see the backlash on Wells Fargo? It's wonderful to watch the public no longer buy this bank's inexcusable racism.

> *"The unfortunate reality is that Wells Fargo paid $175 million to settle claims that it systematically discriminated against Black and Latino home buyers," said the Public Citizen nonprofit group on Twitter.*

> *"Perhaps it's the CEO of Wells Fargo who lacks the talent to recruit black workers," tweeted Representative Alexandria Ocasio-Cortez, a New York Democrat.*

> *"There's plenty of Black talent," said Ohio Democratic Senator Sherrod Brown. "They just don't have the talent for fraud and abuse you're looking for."* [5]

We're at a beautiful time in this country where public corrections are swift for those who try to bypass racial accountability. That's a sign of progress, but we need more white leaders to make bold statements, instead of depending on people of color to fight for ourselves. Pushing back on CEOs and Corporate leaders should not be the responsibility of the oppressed!

GET RID OF THE GATEKEEPERS

Wealth and power in Corporate are carefully guarded. The ascension of brown and Black professionals into the C-Suite, or even through the front door, gets blocked primarily by two departments. Gatekeepers don't often get named as such, but in this case, we must specify who they are and demand accountability.

Let's start with Human Resources, an ongoing pain point for people of color in business. This department serves a primary gatekeeper function and is filled with power-hungry, white women, hellbent on using their opinions and perspectives to influence hiring, firing, raises, and promotions. No one trusts HR. People of color will not risk their careers to be open with an HR person–ever. And thank God we've learned this over the years because in my experience, it was rare to find an HR person with the courage to do what's right. They're put in place to defend Good Ole Boys culture, not to serve the people as a whole.

Brown and Black employment candidates have made monumental efforts to get networked in with HR professionals. When it comes to returning phone calls, responding to emails, and taking our interview requests seriously, HR is the absolute worst. Our words fall on deaf ears, and we are never prioritized. As a result, we don't even try to enter an organization through HR anymore. They do us zero favors.

When we talk about HR being gatekeepers, it's because they often determine who is "qualified" to advance in interviews. Their opinions about people stretch into the business world as well. And it's a shame because most of them have never been taught cultural competency. When they're interviewing a Black woman, they do an apples-to-apples comparison with white candidates. They don't take into account that her achievements were completed with shackles on her feet, living in a racist society, nor do they see her rare insight and resilience. If she can accomplish X with those heavy burdens, imagine if she was released from those burdens, or even just properly supported in business—the levels she could reach with her work ethic and ability to compartmentalize.

Black women work harder than any group I've ever seen, yet it's still often assumed by HR, in particular, that we're among the laziest and most aggressive. All it takes is for one recruiter to whisper to other recruiters outside of the company, and just like that—blackballing occurs for anyone who presents a challenge to dominant culture.

Recruiters are notorious for using veiled language. Their comments about employment candidates of color will lean towards, "I really liked this person," which is often code for, "They aren't threatening," or "They'll fit in enough." It also means this person will not challenge their privilege or make white people uncomfortable. This disadvantages brown and Black people who have foreign accents, direct communication styles, non-American attire, or darker skin. To be seen as a viable candidate, we have to downplay our customs and code switch just to get through the gates.

There is no question that brown and Black people have far more tragic experiences in life. Our ability to articulate the recovery from these circumstances reveals a lot about us. If hiring managers were diverse and woke, they'd naturally see we're just as qualified, if not more so, than someone with copious degrees, titles, and privilege. White people have life challenges, but there's a striking difference in the resources they've had to help them recover. An HR executive with cultural competency will be able to truly make the best choice in a candidate, not based on meritocracy, but rather on character. This is what's sorely missing from the recruiting process.

Human Resources has cost businesses millions of dollars in unqualified candidates. They've also caused truly competent people to be bypassed for jobs. While searching indeed.com, a job website with millions of users, I couldn't find even one Corporate recruiting post in Seattle that had "cultural competency" as a requirement. That's a threat to diverse candidates AND to a company's legal team and profitability. Why should a company pay good money for recruiters and HR teams who can't properly assess talent of color? Why are these people still getting jobs when they're missing vital skills?

The ultimate way to handle HR's oppressive influence is to get rid of the department completely. Consider them wasted overhead. Instead, choose to stand up Black and brown-owned businesses that solve specific business problems–like how to engage in ethical and effective recruiting. I mean, let's face it, there are tasks HR should never have touched in the first place, such as climate and racial temperature surveys.

It only makes sense to have an outside, diverse business poll the company's marginalized employees to identify problematic people and situations. Annual climate surveys might aim for the core of an issue, but people of color do not trust HR to manage their information without it coming back to hurt them. When HR conducts these surveys, real problems are rarely ever addressed. Outsourcing allows the company to get specific feedback, and it lets them funnel money in the direction of diversity.

A DIVERSITY STATEMENT THAT MATTERS

Outsourcing HR to Black and brown owned businesses will also ensure the company's "diversity statement" isn't just a passive commitment. We all know diversity statements rarely translate to real change within a company. I tell my Corporate clients, if they want to make a diversity statement, announce they are no longer tolerating bigotry and abuse of power. Then explain in detail how you intend to deal with the inequities and injustices. Having outside support from a stand-alone, diverse company can allow the business to make a diversity statement that people can actually grasp and get behind.

In a riveting article from *Wired*, "Black Tech Employees Rebel Against 'Diversity Theater'," they examine the annual ritual of diversity reports and how the apology for missing their goals "usually comes from a chief diversity officer—often one of the few nonwhite executives at the company in the first place."[6]

"We aren't where we'd like to be," Facebook's chief diversity officer, Maxine Williams, wrote in 2017. "We continue to have challenges," she wrote the next year. In 2018, she was one of only nine Black females among Facebook's top 1,053 executives."[7]

In Summer 2020, two Black women Pinterest employees, Aerica Shimizu Banks and Ifeoma Ozoma, tweeted that they were "underpaid, threatened, and harassed by colleagues at Pinterest, even as the company tweeted support for Black Lives Matter." Banks worked on the public policy team where she was applauded for her advocacy initiatives, up to a point. Banks eventually touched a nerve with the powers that be and was scolded in her performance review.[8]

"Oh, here's our diversity champion," she says, describing how she felt tokenized by the company. "Here's our expert in this area. Here's our figurehead. But we don't actually want her to do the work we've hired her to do. Way before I spoke out publicly I was speaking up internally, and I was punished for it," she says.[9]

What's happening at Pinterest is commonplace in Corporate America. Diversity leaders, hiring managers, and HR executives should not be internal positions because even the great ones can barely do their jobs while embedded in GOB culture. Outsourcing these positions to independent, Black and brown businesses lets your company handle oppressive matters with mastery.

Having an internal team drive such big changes is downright messy. Allow outside experts with lived experience in racial oppression to take over the (many) tasks of HR.

CLEAR OUT MIDDLE MANAGEMENT

Another pain point for people of color resides at the middle management rank. There are a few opportunities for us to reach this level, but upon arrival, they either plummet or get dragged out for years. Middle management, along with HR, is where generational wealth is being actively destroyed for brown and Black people. There are many facets to this racist dynamic, which I'll continue to explain.

Last week, during a speech at a large tech company, I was asked if it made more sense to have diversity at the top of the company pyramid, rather than middle management. I told them it's important to have diversity modeled in every department, but middle management is where the most racism occurs because they are the gatekeepers of power and access. Here are some examples for you:

Most companies do annual **performance reviews** on employees, but beforehand, there's a process called **calibration**, which I led in my Corporate positions. Calibration puts the performance of the organization into a bell curve. So there's 10% on the bottom, then it goes up to where most employees fall. Expectations of them are being met. On the other side of the bell curve are the performers. These are the ones getting higher annual salaries and bonuses, while the low side of the curve usually doesn't get an increase, but rather gets put on a **performance improvement plan (PIP)** that will last 60-90 days.

Middle management tells the employee what they need to do to improve, and in most cases, their standards are both unfair and unrealistic because those who fall on the bottom 10% are often brown and Black people. It's a setup to ultimately ditch us, and HR does nothing to help.

The PIP has become the 911 system in Corporate America. White people use 911 as a weapon to get rescued, secure dominance, and manufacture threats by a Black person. It creates a false narrative about the Black individual, and the legitimacy of the white person calling the cops is never in question, except when there's a *video* proving they've been racist. In Corporate America, there are no videos, but there is a vehicle used to tear apart brown and Black people's lives. It's called the PIP.

You see, when a brown or Black person's performance is low, there's no unbiased or informed party to assess the duress, abuse, and mental anguish this person has had to face in the workplace. No one is probing to see how that person's troubled performance correlates to the environment the manager is creating. White middle management, along with HR, makes the rules and writes the script. This explains why brown and Black people struggle to succeed with these oppressive leaders. Managers should receive feedback to identify their own growing edge. They should be put on a timeline for improvement and fired if they can't improve. Corporate America, when does your Performance Improvement Plan begin? See how it feels to have 90 days to become something or someone you are not!

Succession planning is another area of Corporate racism. It occurs when middle management comes together to list future candidates for key positions in the organization. Current employees are evaluated for competency and potential, and diverse people are required to be on this list.

From there, a two-to-four year **development plan** is created for the upcoming leaders in question.

As an HR leader, I found myself bringing succession plans forward each time there were job openings. I'd contact decision makers to see how development plans were going with their diverse candidates. Over the years, I saw white, middle management leaders had no intention of promoting the company's brown and Black candidates. Oftentimes, when opportunities for advancement would arise, middle management would select external candidates and claim the requirements for this position had changed. To further string along the candidate of color, they'd sometimes extend that person's development plan from two-to-four years, to four-to-five.

Any time a brown or Black person is considered for leadership, it's nearly impossible for them to fit the ever-changing requirements from middle management. I'd often try to work with diverse employees to add scope to their profile, but they'd rightfully get frustrated when advancement was given away, and they were never viewed as being good enough or right enough to qualify.

Adding diverse people onto succession plans is a "check the box" activity that doesn't fulfill our ability to rise. It's an exercise in pleasing the CEO that fails to promote folx who are prime for those upgraded positions. Because of that, brown and Black executives will often leave the organization before the fulfillment of their development plan because they are sick of being lied to, ignored, and abused.

As I'm writing this, Republicans in Georgia just passed a horribly racist law. They now restrict water distribution to people standing in voting lines and have removed mail-in registrations and remote voting.[10] Republicans did that because they lost the election in Georgia and are losing their foothold on white supremacy in the South. Their efforts were meant to punish brown and Black voters and take away our strength. That is exactly what Corporate does with succession plans. It's just another manifestation of those in power clinging to white privilege. They can't stand the thought of a person of color "showing them up."

Succession planning conjures an environment of in-fighting and backstabbing. It makes sense, too, right? People want security and access to the land of the lucrative. The whole environment is downright toxic.

Racial progress in Corporate will never happen until the gatekeepers are named, addressed, removed, and replaced. Companies can start by requiring middle management numbers to match the same percentage of brown and Black people that reside in their area. That will give them a tangible number for promoting or appointing people of color into levels directly below the CEO, which can be VP or Director level jobs. This is where the equity in the company is generously offered. It's where people of color deserve to be because diversity now equals profits, and even more so, it's a way for us all to rise and be cared for collectively. The challenges continue to mount, though, particularly in our quest for equal pay.

OPEN THE GATES OF POWER AND WEALTH

When we talk about **pay equity** and **pay transparency**, we're pointing fingers in the wrong direction. We're actually ignoring a much bigger source of extreme wealth in Corporate. Middle management gates aren't guarded because of the enormity of **base salaries**. They are guarded because there are megabucks to be made in **stocks** and **bonuses**, which are only offered to middle and upper management. This massive source of inequity is what everyone should be talking about and scrutinizing.

To help you understand **earning power**, I googled Sheryl Sandberg's total compensation, which was roughly $27 million, yet her base salary at Facebook is around $800K.[11] That shows how much "upside" potential she has to her base salary. Her stock options alone launch her into the multi-million dollar category and could be worth hundreds of millions if the stock does well.

Black folx cannot build wealth on straight salaries. We should be able to see the ladder of progress, where equity grants begin and success can look somewhat linear. Rarely do we achieve these levels. For us, it's never a straight line!

Full transparency on **total compensation** for middle and upper management must come to the forefront. Brown and Black people should be taught how to understand "**salary structures**" and the benefits afforded only to top people. This helps us see where we are being placed, and if we're on par with others, particularly our white counterparts.

Let me demonstrate how important this is: Companies use **stock options** and **restricted stock** to retain and attract top tier management and high performing talent. Stock options provide the possibility of a "big payday" if the company's stock soars.

Say an executive receives 5000 stock options at a $5.00 exercise price. An exercise price is the option to purchase a given number of shares. The exercise price is determined by Fair Market Value at the time the options are granted. These stock grants are designed as a "retention sort of method" to keep the executive working for a defined period of time. If the grant is provided over a period of time, it is an incentive. The grant may be valued at about $10,000. However, if the stock soars to $100 and you have 5,000 shares: $95.00 x 5000 shares = $475,000. Imagine if brown and Black people by the masses had access to this "generational wealth" building opportunity.

Restricted stock are shares of the company that vest or become available to an employee over time. They are restricted, meaning they cannot be sold until the shares vest. So, say you're given 5000 restricted shares and four years before the options fully become available. If the vesting schedule is 25% each year, you would be able to draw the 25% vested money each year, adding an extra yearly income.

See how that works? This is why there's a fight to keep brown and Black professionals out of these levels of wealth and management. It's where the bulk of the money resides. Here's another issue:

Aside from not having access to stocks and bonuses, brown and Black professionals are still getting screwed in the salary department. To explain, we're going to crunch a few more numbers and throw around some Corporate jargon. Whatever you don't fully understand, allow yourself research. I'm revealing "inside secrets" you need to know. It's a lot to absorb, and I commend you for educating yourself.

For most of my career, I saw many brown and Black people at a .70 **compa-ratio** or below, which is the salary percentage against the market. This means their salary is 30%+ below the market. **Salary structures** typically move three, five, or 10% per year. This means the person of color's salary that's 30%+ below market will never catch up to their full market salary. Gone are the days when people would stay in the same positions for years with a minimal three percent salary increase. While the economy is rising at hypothetically 25%, that measly three percent is an insult. This needs to be a major talking point in the equity conversation.

We also need to talk about **401(k) retirement contributions which are dependent on salaries.** Therefore, the practice of keeping people down in salary range compounds broader, total compensation, bonus pools, equity, grants, and retirement. In addition, senior executives often participate in "senior executive retirement plans" (SERPs) which provide benefits over and above what is available to other employees. Are you feeling how significant these issues are and how they are contributing to lack of generational wealth?

Another term you'll need to know to crush Corporate racism is **change in control agreements**, which middle management executives and higher levels often negotiate before accepting their position. Change in control agreements (sometimes called **change *of* control**) provide terms and arrangements of protection if the company changes hands or shifts leadership due to a merger, acquisition, or other event. Shareholders typically benefit from these situations, while the very people whose hard work led to this profitable change are not rewarded. In some cases, they're left out entirely, lose their jobs or are placed in vulnerable positions.

Change in control agreements tighten the noose on Corporate America and make it harder to fire us. Executives can usually negotiate one to two years of full pay, plus bonuses. That's both a safety net and a source of peace. Change in control agreements should be required for every brown and Black employee and should include not just change in control from leadership, but when leadership no longer deems them acceptable in the workplace.

This kind of security keeps people off social systems, welfare, and food stamps. It allows them to retain medical insurance and helps brown and Black professionals keep up their earning power, so we don't risk unemployment and losing our homes. Because we're disproportionately fired and labeled performance problems, there's a ripple effect in our lives for years following these big changes. It isn't easy to just get another job when the dark network is snubbing you behind the scenes. If there had been a change in control agreement in place for me, it would have prevented my litigation costs and helped me land on my feet. Instead, it's taken me nearly a decade to find solid ground.

CORPORATE'S ABILITY TO AFFECT THE MASSES

How is Corporate going to pay back for the generational and psychological harm it has done to brown and Black people? To wrap up this chapter, let's talk about **Corporate philanthropy** dollars.

Charity Navigator reported that 70% of charitable giving comes through individual donors. Only 5% is attributed to Corporate philanthropy.[12] What? Those numbers are abysmal. Corporate America has the ability to create large-scale, monumental changes for people of color. It would mean heavily investing in marginalized communities—not just a little, but as a massive and ongoing priority.

Corporate philanthropy likes to vary their donations and brag about the "feel good" nonprofits they choose like pet shelters. But when Black kids or displaced people of color are the primary benefactors, enthusiasm and support are minimal. Equity says you must invest *more* into communities of color. If anything, the kids deserve our help. Public education is continually underfunded and defunded, and is failing brown and Black kids miserably all over the country.

Seattle Seahawks quarterback Russell Wilson and singer Ciara started a tuition-free, public charter school in Des Moines, Washington. They donated $1.75 million to re-brand the existing charter known as Cascade Midway Academy. The couple said the school will focus "on academics, personalized student plans and internships and mentorships for underserved Black and brown students."[13]

We need more contributions like that because public education tells our kids they will never make it, they aren't deep thinkers, or they won't cut it for college—all while teaching them a white-washed and untrue version of American history. They also try to divert kids of color into careers with lower earning power.

Affluent, white families who don't like their kids' teachers or who disagree with the curriculum can afford to move districts or transfer to private schools. Wealthy, white parents will pay thousands to have SAT scores inflated to ensure their kid's success. Actress Felicity Huffman was recently one of 50 people charged with fabricating test scores and athletic ability of prominent kids for smoother entry into elite colleges.[14]

The issue of education is maddening because government dollars are limited, unions are heavily involved, and this issue has sadly turned political. Republicans want money going to charter schools, while Democrats keep pushing for public education to be improved. And yet, neither one is completely solving the true problem. Here's why:

> "A recent report from a nonprofit called EdBuild found that on average, predominantly white school districts receive $23 billion more in funding than school districts that primarily serve students of color and those from low-income families (the difference is largely due to local wealth and taxes.)"[15] So if Democrats and the unions get their way, the same financial trend will continue, and if Republicans win out, the charter schools *they* endorse will keep excluding brown and Black kids. Without access to schools that harness teachers of color

and learning environments conducive to minority students, it's pointless to continue believing public schools will do their job for our children.

The government's "back and forth" partisan fight over education keeps both the conversations and solutions stagnant. They keep employing the same unsuccessful strategies over and over, which is literally the definition of insanity. It's time to stop this pattern and stop pretending the government is going to change at all. Corporations have the means to funnel millions into the education, health, and stability of their future workforce. Corporate America should be *owning* education as an initiative, and beyond that, CEOs should be shoveling their own millions towards education.

My suggestion is to follow Russell Wilson and Ciara's example and fund private schools that are led by brown and Black people–schools that don't cost a dime to families. Fixing education also means kids having *access* to education. Wouldn't it make sense to offer free Wifi to brown and Black homes regardless of location? Corporate can make this part of their benefits package for employees.

The pandemic changed office and school life as we know it. Corporate has the chance right now to make an enormous statement about access to education. This would show Corporate's investment not only in minority education, but in the community as a whole. Corporate's tax structure gives them every break in the world. They can afford this, believe me. Wealth distribution only widened during the pandemic. While the masses suffered with unemployment and uncertainty, CEOs made a killing!

People don't realize Corporate's power to fix society's biggest issues—education, housing, health care, and taxes. They have buckets of philanthropy dollars, as well as the ability to change the oppressive policies that affect the marginalized. For instance, banks could eliminate credit scores, which would open the floodgates for diverse people to secure homes, cars, and access to education. People have no idea how much POWER companies have. When it comes to their future workforce, why shouldn't they be responsible?

YOU HOLD THE KEYS TO CORPORATE TRANSFORMATION

Remember, this book is meant to be a starting point in crushing Corporate racism. If the jargon is new to you, that's okay. People spend years in Corporate without seeing behind the curtain and learning the lingo. Performance improvement plans (PIP), succession planning, change in control agreements, development plans—these are the tools of white supremacy in Corporate. Pay equity, pay transparency, earning power, stock options, and total cash compensation—these are the terms you need to know to get in this battle. White people will use this information for their own gain.

That's a given. But please remember, the goal is to improve the lives of brown and Black people. We are the priority!

You've been given the key areas of racism to examine in your community, your workplace, and the world of politics. These changes might not happen overnight, but one thing's for sure—you'll never look at Corporate protocol and philanthropy the same. You cannot unsee what you just read here, so get conversations started in your professional and personal circles. Hire brown and Black experts like me to help you evolve as quickly and effectively as possible.

There's no time to waste!

"Take this wineskin
My spirit burst for something new
There's nothing I want more than you
Cuz only you can satisfy"

–Hillsong United, "Water to Wine"

6

A CALL FOR COURAGE

My goal in this book was to demonstrate the systems of racism in Corporate America and beyond. We started with my firing at Financial Services Inc. and the debilitating trial that followed. Most people, after winning a lawsuit, would have taken the money, paid off their bills, and secured another decent paying job. That wasn't an option for me, and not because I couldn't get hired. I refused to endure another round of abuse. I wanted to tell the truth, speak unapologetically, create something meaningful, and have the courage to simply be. Like for many Black women entrepreneurs, building my own business hasn't been easy, but the Corporate alternative is even worse. This book taught you how to start fixing that, or at least how to start the right conversations.

This book is a conduit of liberty for my brown and Black readers. To each of you I send my heartfelt love. I see your struggles and hope you feel validated and supported like never before. Oppression, at the hands of greed, will no longer be tolerated. Our days as tokens of injustice in Good Ole Boys culture are coming to an end. White women are being called to the carpet, and bigoted leaders are quickly losing their prominence. In the wake of this racial reckoning, every organization is going to have to face class action lawsuits by classes of people. The rates at which people of color are (and have been) reduced will become headlines. Mark my words. It's a new day in which we are unleashed by the blood of our ancestors who picked cotton and built this country brick by brick. We deserve to live well and have lucrative careers. We deserve to be safe and respected. Make no mistake, this book was created for you.

To my white readers, I hope you feel humbled and inspired to make personal changes, while pushing for collective change. This book was meant to empower you--because when you're able to see oppression, you no longer can be clueless, innocent, shocked, or appalled by the rare instances you do see. You'll understand, right away, it's an everyday occurrence in America that must shift immediately. My hope is that you stop shutting down important conversations and welcome new learning at every opportunity--that you start being role models for racial progress and disruptors of damaging policies.

Other countries value rest and balance. If Corporate America can't ease up on the pressure to perform, they can at least direct some of that energy to dismantling their racially abusive systems. Antiracism work isn't comfortable, but neither is the current state of affairs. Each of us must commit to building resilience and committing to self-care.

Beyond my Epsom salt baths and a soothing glass of Syrah, I find solace in my faith, friends, and vision for Corporate America that can radically shift the wealth and stability of brown and Black folx. Alone, we continue to struggle. Together, we can move mountains. Personal, professional, and global transformation can occur faster than you think. Yet the question always remains, "Corporate America, do you have the COURAGE to change?"

NOTES

FOREWORD

1. Tupac Shakur, "Can U C the Pride in the Panther," in *The Rose That Grew from Concrete* (New York: Pocket Books, 1999), 127.

2. Tupac Shakur, "Ambitionz az a Ridah," track # 1 on All Eyez on Me, Death Row Records and Interscope Records, 1996, compact disc.

3. Tupac Shakur and Talent, "Changes," track # 5 on Greatest Hits (disc 2), Amaru Entertainment, Death Row Records, and Interscope Records, 1998, compact disc.

INTRODUCTION

1. Cheryl Dorsey, Jeff Bradach, and Peter Kim, "Racial Equity and Philanthropy" (The Bridgespan

Group, Echoing Green, May 4, 2020), https://www.bridgespan.org/insights/library/philanthropy/disparities-nonprofit-funding-for-leaders-of-color.

CHAPTER 2

1. Farida D., Instagram post, January 10, 2021, https://www.instagram.com/p/CJ304_LMS3w/.

2. Chris Perez, "Jerry Jones: Cowboys Players Will Be Benched for 'Disrespecting' the Flag," *New York Post*, October 9, 2017, https://nypost.com/2017/10/08/jerry-jones-cowboys-players-will-be-benched-for-disrespecting-the-flag/.

3. Laura Morgan Roberts and Anthony J. Mayo, "Toward a Racially Just Workplace," *Harvard Business Review*, November 14, 2019, https://hbr.org/2019/11/toward-a-racially-just-workplace.

4. "Quantifying America's Gender Wage Gap by Race/Ethnicity" (National Partnership For Women & Families, March 2021), https://www.nationalpartnership.org/our-work/resources/economic-justice/fair-pay/quantifying-americas-gender-wage-gap.pdf.

5. "Quantifying America's Gender Wage Gap."

6. Roberts and Mayo, "Toward a Racially Just Workplace."

CHAPTER 3

1. *The Reflections of Race | Cindi Bright | TEDx-ColoradoSprings*, TEDxTalks (Colorado Springs, CO, 2019), https://www.youtube.com/watch?v=et9RO7dgs4o.

7. Erica Chayes Wida, "What Does 'Reverse Racism' Mean and Is It Actually Real? Experts Weigh In," *Today*, June 26, 2020, https://www.today.com/tmrw/what-reverse-racism-experts-weigh-term-t184580.

8. Wida, "What Does 'Reverse Racism' Mean."

CHAPTER 4

1. Sheryl Sandberg and Nell Scovell, *Lean in: Women, Work, and the Will to Lead* (New York: Alfred A. Knopf, 2013).

2. Connie Schultz, "Review: Sheryl Sandberg's 'Lean In' Is Full of Good Intentions, but Rife with Contradictions," *Washington Post*, March 1, 2013, sec. Opinions, https://www.washingtonpost.com/opinions/review-sheryl-sandbergs-lean-in-is-full-of-good-intentions-but-rife-with-contradictions/2013/03/01/3380e00e-7f9a-11e2-a350-49866afab584_story.html.

3. "Quantifying America's Gender Wage Gap by Race/Ethnicity" (National Partnership For Women & Families, March 2021), https://www.nationalpartnership.org/our-work/resources/economic-

justice/fair-pay/quantifying-americas-gender-wage-gap.pdf.

4. Emma Hinchliffe, "The Number of Women Running Fortune 500 Companies Hits an All-Time Record," *Fortune*, May 18, 2020, https://fortune.com/2020/05/18/women-ceos-fortune-500-2020/.

5. Walter Loeb, "Roz Brewer Is New CEO Of Walgreens," *Forbes*, January 29, 2021, https://www.forbes.com/sites/walterloeb/2021/01/29/roz-brewer-is-new-ceo-of-walgreens/.

6. Richard Pérez-Peña, "Woman Linked to 1955 Emmett Till Murder Tells Historian Her Claims Were False," *The New York Times*, January 28, 2017, sec. U.S., https://www.nytimes.com/2017/01/27/us/emmett-till-lynching-carolyn-bryant-donham.html.

7. Christian Cooper, "Central Park this morning: this woman's dog is tearing through the plantings in the Ramble. ME: Ma'am, dogs in the Ramble have to be on the leash at all times.," Facebook post, May 25, 2020, https://www.facebook.com/christian.cooper1/posts/10158742137255229.

8. Amir Vera and Laura Ly, "White Woman Who Called Police on a Black Man Bird-Watching in Central Park Has Been Fired," *CNN*, May 26, 2020, https://www.cnn.com/2020/05/26/us/central-park-video-dog-video-african-american-trnd/index.html.

9. Personal Service Agreement between the University of Connecticut and Robin DiAngelo, LLC., June 4, 2020. Signed document obtained by the author showing the University of Connecticut agreed to pay a $20,000 speaking fee and up to $2,000 in travel expenses.

10. Anastasia Reesa Tomkin, "How White People Conquered the Nonprofit Industry," *Nonprofit Quarterly*, May 26, 2020, https://nonprofitquarterly.org/how-white-people-conquered-the-nonprofit-industry/.

11. Cheryl Dorsey, Jeff Bradach, and Peter Kim, "Racial Equity and Philanthropy" (The Bridgespan Group, Echoing Green, May 4, 2020), https://www.bridgespan.org/insights/library/philanthropy/disparities-nonprofit-funding-for-leaders-of-color.

12. Courtney Connley, "How Stacey Abrams, LaTosha Brown and Other Black Women Changed the Course of the 2020 Election," *CNBC*, November 6, 2020, https://www.cnbc.com/2020/11/06/black-women-continue-to-be-the-democratic-partys-most-powerful-weapon.html.

CHAPTER 5

1. Vivian Hunt et al., "Delivering through Diversity" (McKinsey & Company, January 2018), https://www.mckinsey.com/~/media/mckinsey/busi-

ness%20functions/organization/our%20insights/
delivering%20through%20diversity/delivering-
through-diversity_full-report.ashx

2. Max Larkin, "Cornel West, Feeling 'Disrespect-
   ed,' Is Leaving Harvard For A Second Time,"
   WBUR, March 8, 2021, https://www.wbur.org/
   edify/2021/03/08/cornel-west-leaving-harvard.

3. David Kroman, "Revered Doctor Steps down,
   Accusing Seattle Children's Hospital of Racism,"
   Crosscut, December 31, 2020, https://crosscut.
   com/equity/2020/12/revered-doctor-steps-down-
   accusing-seattle-childrens-hospital-racism.

4. John Biers, "Wells Fargo CEO Sorry For 'In-
   sensitive' Comments On Race," September 23,
   2020, *Barron's,* https://www.barrons.com/news/
   wells-fargo-ceo-sorry-for-insensitive-comments-on-
   race-01600886406.

5. Biers, "Wells Fargo CEO Sorry."

6. Sidney Fussell, "Black Tech Employees Rebel
   Against 'Diversity Theater,'" *Wired*, March 8, 2021,
   https://www.wired.com/story/black-tech-employ-
   ees-rebel-against-diversity-theater/.

7. Fussell, "Black Tech Employees Rebel."

8. Fussell, "Black Tech Employees Rebel."

9. Fussell, "Black Tech Employees Rebel."

10. Nick Corasaniti, "Georgia G.O.P. Passes Major Law to Limit Voting Amid Nationwide Push," *The New York Times*, March 25, 2021, sec. U.S., https://www.nytimes.com/2021/03/25/us/politics/georgia-voting-law-republicans.html.

11. "Compensation Information for Sheryl K. Sandberg, COO of Facebook Inc," Salary.com, accessed April 13, 2021, https://www1.salary.com/Sheryl-K-Sandberg-Salary-Bonus-Stock-Options-for-FACE-BOOK-INC.html.

12. "Giving Statistics," Charity Navigator, accessed April 13, 2021, http://www.charitynavigator.org/index.cfm?bay=content.view&cpid=42.

13. Madeline Coleman, "Russell Wilson, Ciara to Fund Public Charter School South of Seattle," *Sports Illustrated*, October 29, 2020, https://www.si.com/nfl/2020/10/29/russell-wilson-ciara-fund-public-charter-school-seattle.

14. Tom Winter et al., "Lori Loughlin, Felicity Huffman among 50 Charged in College Admissions Scheme," *NBC News,* March 12, 2019, https://www.nbcnews.com/news/us-news/feds-uncover-massive-college-entrance-exam-cheating-plot-n982136.

15. P. R. Lockhart, "What the College Admissions Scandal Says about Racial Inequality," *Vox*, March 20, 2019, https://www.vox.com/identities/2019/3/20/18271462/college-admissions-race-stuyvesant-affirmative-action-inequality.

ABOUT CINDI BRIGHT

Fearless and candid, Cindi Bright aims to reimagine prosperity for all. She is a keynote speaker, Corporate consultant, TEDx presenter, and radio host. Marked as a woman to lead transfiguration in Corporate America, she boldly uses her voice to propel change. Inspired by Deepak Chopra's Soul of Leadership executive course, she completed her Executive MBA from Foster School of Business, University of Washington. Cindi currently resides in Bellevue, Washington.